Conversations
with
Marilyn

Conversations with Marilyn

W. J. WEATHERBY

PARAGON
HOUSE

Paragon House paperback edition, 1992

Published in the United States by
Paragon House Publishers
90 Fifth Avenue
New York, N.Y. 10011

Library of Congress Cataloging-in-Publication Data

Weatherby, William J.
        Conversations with Marilyn / W.J. Weatherby.
                p.   cm.
        Originally published: New York : Mason/Charter, 1976.
        ISBN 1-55778-512-0
        1. Monroe, Marilyn, 1926-1962.   2. Motion picture actors
and actresses—United States—Biography.   I. Title.
        [PN2287.M69W4 1992]
        791.43'028'092—dc20
        [B]   91-43173
                                                                        CIP

To
Kathleen Weatherby
and
James Monroe Parker
and
Tyrone Romell Braggs
and
Norman Folsom

"You're right about her not being easy to know. One *sees* her, with intensity—sees her more than one sees almost any one; but then one discovers that that isn't knowing her and that one may know better a person whom one doesn't 'see,' as I say, half so well."

—Henry James, *The Wings of the Dove*

INTRODUCTION TO THE PARAGON HOUSE EDITION

A publisher once told me, "There are three subjects of unending interest—John Kennedy, Ernest Hemingway, and Marilyn Monroe."

Kennedy and Hemingway have certainly survived their revisionist critics and are regularly written about, but perhaps Marilyn Monroe is the most popular of all, still a living legend in this, the thirtieth year since her death.

In 1976, in reviewing the first edition of this book in the *Washington Post*, Larry McMurtry wrote that Marilyn had been dead almost fifteen years, "but somehow her presence still haunts the national consciousness. She is right in there with our major ghosts: Hemingway, the Kennedy brothers—people who finished with American life before America had time to finish with them."

How much truer that seems sixteen years later in 1992.

Her beauty, her mischievousness, and her mastery of the film medium have made her later movies—over which she had some control—into timeless classics. Sybil Thorndike, the great English actress, who appeared with her in *The Prince and the Showgirl*, told me Marilyn's acting didn't seem remarkable when you were with her in the studio, but when you saw her on the screen you realized what a great movie actress she was.

That was enough to explain her popularity in her lifetime, but not perhaps her even greater popularity since her

i

death. It is when you add her uniquely vulnerable quality, so vividly revealed on screen and off, the quality that made possible the mystery of her death, that her hold on so many people's affection for so long seems quite understandable. In her lifetime there were many acquaintances who were so moved by her wistful loneliness that they thought it was their mission to save her from those who would take advantage of her, and obviously she still stirs such protective feelings in people even though she is no longer here to be saved.

I have always been impressed by the sheer variety of her admirers ranging from older people who were her contemporaries—Marilyn would have been in her late sixties today—to young people who were not even born when she died on August 4, 1962. Fans of different ages, social backgrounds, and nationalities have written to me requesting a meeting so that they could talk to someone who knew her. It was as close as they could get to her. Such fans also take photographs of the buildings she lived in and the Actors' Studio where she studied with Lee and Paula Strasberg.

I remember one teenager wrote to me from a remote village in Ireland asking the most personal questions about her and describing at length how much Marilyn had influenced her life. And of course her admirers have not just been unknown fans at a posthumous distance. When she was alive, she attracted such complex and quite different celebrity figures as John and Robert Kennedy, Joe DiMaggio and Arthur Miller.

When I interviewed Saul Bellow after he was awarded the Nobel Prize for Literature, the formality of our exchanges was only overcome when we discovered we were both great admirers of Marilyn. "Ah, I liked her so much," said Bellow. "She was a nice lady. So witty." I like to quote that to people—and there are still some left—who put her down in death as they did in life as a childish, dumb blonde. The same scoffers dismiss John Kennedy's effect on the America of his time as mere public relations and Hemingway's image as that of a macho monster. But such simplifications fail to account for the profound influence these "major ghosts" continue to have on us.

I reread this book thinking perhaps there might be some updating to do. But the truth is all that was a mystery about her when I wrote this book still remains a mystery. We are still unsure about the relationship she had with President Kennedy and Robert Kennedy. We still don't know how she died—whether it was of an accidental drug overdose, or whether it was suicide or even murder. Suicide seems out of character for the Marilyn I knew, and much of the circumstantial evidence suggesting she was killed may be simply due to the cover-ups and conspiracies of silence that always occur when major political figures or Mafia leaders or corrupt union leaders are involved in a potentially scandalous situation, and all three played a role in Marilyn's last days. President Kennedy had apparently shared a Mafia leader's mistress and Jimmy Hoffa of the Teamsters wanted to get something on Robert Kennedy: Marilyn was a mere pawn in this power play. President Kennedy was killed just over a year after her death and exactly how that came about also remains a mystery. With so many of the people who knew the truth no longer alive thirty years later, it is unlikely we shall ever solve the mystery of Marilyn's death—or Kennedy's.

But my intention when I wrote this book was not to play investigative reporter but simply to portray the Marilyn I came to know through conversations with her.

I saw recently the few scenes she made before being

fired on her last uncompleted movie, *Something's Got to Give*. She played a wife who comes home after a long absence to discover her husband thought she was dead and has married again. She was often amusing in her own touching way, but her face lacked the youthful fullness it used to have and showed instead the drawn look of someone in whom age and anguish were beginning to show through the makeup. She feared she would eventually have a breakdown and end in a mental home like her mother. Old age would have been particularly hard for her. She might have died a broken old woman like Garbo, a legend still but not so beloved. Instead dying as she did at thirty-six, close to her prime, she will be forever that mischievous, vulnerable, beautiful blonde who haunts the American dream.

I reached much the same conclusion when I wrote this book. But one further appeal of Marilyn's occurs to me now after the public deceptions of the last thirty years. Unlike other major ghosts who have been put on lofty pedestals, she never tried to suppress the truth about herself. The suppressions in her life, especially at the end, were all to protect the public reputations of others. Perhaps Marilyn is still remembered so warmly today because she allowed herself to be wholly known, warts and all. It makes her seem very rare and refreshing.

W.J.W.

1

Most of this book is based on two dusty, fading old short-hand notebooks that contained accounts of long conversations I had with Marilyn Monroe toward the end of her life.

I first met her in Reno in 1960, two years before she died, when she was making what was to be her last movie, *The Misfits*. I was a newspaper reporter covering the event. She knew then that we were meeting so that I could write about her, and she was suitably cautious—or as cautious as she ever was. But later, when I came to know her better in New York, we met on the understanding that we were talking privately and that I wouldn't write about it, at least not then, and she was more relaxed and forthcoming.

We used to meet in a bar on Eighth Avenue, a plain place made for real drinkers who liked their money's worth in the glass and didn't care much about the surroundings; not a place where you would expect to find a movie star. She was invariably in disguise, usually wearing a head scarf, a blouse, sloppy pants, and no makeup. I hadn't recognized her the first time I saw her dressed that way in Reno, and she was seldom recognized in New York when I was with her.

Even though I wasn't using shorthand during our meetings, as a longtime reporter I always made notes of our conversations immediately afterward. In those days, because I had done a long series of interviews with well-known people, my memory was trained to recall long stretches of conversation. I may not always have remembered her exact words, the rhythm of her sentences, but generally I think I did, and her meaning was always accurately noted, even to describing some of her facial reactions. There was no way I could record the tones of that unique voice, however, which could range from the seductive to the girlish to the intonations of a grandame.

When she died I was free to write about our meetings, but, much as I had written about her when she was alive, I had no wish to do so at the end. Perhaps I was afraid of being one of the vultures still feeding off her. Also, like most reporters, I was in full-time pursuit of the living and felt the dead could safely be left to biographers.

But eventually, because the rush of Monroe literature since her death contained little firsthand evidence of what she was like in action—in talk—a publisher asked me if I would take the records of our conversations out of the closet and set down my own impressions. She had an ability, unique in my experience, to appear to be what you wanted her to be and therefore the real person remained elusive. That is why I have kept my own comments to a minimum and tried to let her speak for herself. I once interviewed (it was Marilyn's suggestion) one of the founders of Hollywood—Sam Goldwyn. He told me that I had reported the long interview with him as accurately as "humanly possible." I hope she would have felt the same way about this book.

•

Long before meeting her, I was prejudiced against her. I admired her husband, Arthur Miller, as a serious dramatist—I was, in fact, more interested in him than in her. The famous writer, it seemed to me, was being reduced to no more than an appendage to the famous star, the latest in a line of legendary Hollywood blondes (and the last of the line, though we didn't know it then). I wondered how a marriage to her could possibly survive, and of course it didn't. "Marilyn's husband" went back to being plain Arthur Miller again.

But this prejudice against her was to help me in finding the real person behind the image of Marilyn. It meant that I didn't fall too easily for her professional charm. She herself was painfully aware of the problem. "I carry Marilyn Monroe around with me like an albatross," she told me the last time I saw her. She hadn't even liked the name when a Hollywood studio gave it to her as a young actress after rejecting her real name—Norma Jeane Mortensen—as not glamorous enough. The trouble was, "Marilyn Monroe" was a golden albatross, and although she occasionally took big risks in both her public and private life, she never risked giving up the albatross. Age would have made her do it eventually, but she was gone long before then.

Her feeling about her image explained why she sometimes enjoyed dressing in a way that people couldn't recognize. Although I had been looking out for her the first time, I thought she was a local housewife when she appeared. And the last time in New York—in the drinkers' bar on Eighth Avenue—a man made a similar mistake. While I was away in the men's room, he made a pass at her, thinking she was a prostitute off the avenue. She hadn't been what either of us had expected. All of my conversations with her contained similar surprises, as I hope this book will show.

Yet even while she was enjoying an occasional experience of obscurity, she was also busy furthering her albatross image. It was as if she were in a race she couldn't drop out of—a race to the death. It had become a way of life from which she occasionally revolted, but without success and not for long.

5

When photographers took pictures for the magazines, she acted as censor—and a ruthless one she was. She had posed the way she wanted to appear and she would not release any photographs that didn't do full justice to the superstar. I was present once when a photographer brought her about a hundred photographs of herself; she killed all but about ten of them. She was very shrewd about the marketing of her image—at the same time that another side of her pined for an escape from it. This explains, I think, the extra subtlety in her performances as a Hollywood blonde, beautiful but dumb; she could give the performance expected of her and yet also seem to be mocking herself as a glamor girl.

When people who knew her well talked or wrote about her, they tended to be too defensive, and she invariably came out seeming like the nice blonde girl next door. *Nice* is the last word I'd use for the Marilyn Monroe I knew; it's too colorless and one-dimensional. "I can be a monster," she told me when I asked her why she'd bitched out someone who seemed quite well meaning. She was no more a monster than she was nice; she was many things to many people, and I doubt whether even those who saw most of her, such as her husbands, ever saw her completely without some of her mental makeup on. If you considered her a blonde bombshell, she'd play that for you, but have no respect for you—which was all many people wanted.

In a magazine article I wrote about her last film, I described her various moods, including the bitchiness. Arthur Miller read the article in typescript and asked if he could cut out the reference to her bitchiness. I was touched at the time: it seemed to reflect his deep feeling for her, even though their marriage had broken up. But now it reflects for me the overprotective attitude of those around her, an attitude that furthered

6

the cause of the image, the albatross, at the expense of the real woman's complexity.

She didn't respect ass-kissers of any kind, though she made use of them. If you showed a decent independence and even lack of interest in her, however, she became interested. At least that was my experience of her. She gave me an exclusive interview and was generally very kind to me while she was making her last film. But I still didn't pursue the acquaintance until we met accidentally in New York months later, and again my apparent lack of interest seemed to intrigue her.

I can understand why she sometimes had a drink and a talk with someone who clearly didn't want anything from her (and we had quite a few things in common), but I feel that the other side of her also had in mind that she was giving her time to a professional writer who one day would make use of the experience. Not then, but later. What did she want our conversations to convey? Perhaps a portrait of a complicated woman instead of just another look at the albatross, a woman who could not be labeled or pigeonholed in a group, a profession, or a race. What did it tell you about her to say she was a Californian, a movie star, and white? She was an elusive individual who left unique, heavy memories.

I went to interview Arthur Miller when he was on a short visit to Ireland, just before filming started on *The Misfits*. I had the idea that Ireland was sufficiently outside the rat race to have the right values about artists. I was soon disillusioned. The small town of Galway greeted the playwright the way New York or London would have done. MARILYN'S HUSBAND IN GALWAY, newspaper headlines proclaimed.

Miller was visiting John Huston who had been hired to direct the movie. Huston's Irish home in St. Clerans was hidden in a peaceful Irish landscape of green slopes and lazing horses, like the retreat of the ringleader in a Hollywood thriller. Lillian Ross, in *Picture*, long ago pointed out how, with Mr. Huston, life was apt to get confused with art and everyday events seemed like scenes from a Huston film.

This impression grew in the large library adorned by murals (one was a lonely lighthouse painted by Bernard Buffet) and cluttered with mementoes and current scripts. John Huston had as much of an image as Marilyn Monroe did: his was that of a Hemingway tough guy, sportsman, and bigtime gambler who was also a movie artist, a director with the manner of a great stage actor. The man of action seemed constantly in conflict with the movie man. His looks and actions often seemed to be saying: "What the hell is a tough guy like me doing in the phony effeminate movie world?" But he could deal with the Hollywood moguls and publicity machines as well as Marilyn Monroe did, and if his image was an albatross, too, he seemed better able to escape from it into other roles.

He and his guest, Arthur Miller, both tall, lean men, were the kind of contrast Huston might have cast for a big scene. The host, still on crutches with a leg broken while hunting, was dressed flamboyantly and sat behind a big cigar. He had the sort of expansive charm that can coax good performances from bad actors or enthusiastic backing from ruthless businessmen. In the hall a waiter in a white coat waited patiently behind a bar—a touch of Huston flamboyance in his role of lord of the manor. Arthur Miller sat far back in his chair, an introvert in a white shirt and dark slacks, listening, noting, studying, only occasionally relaxing into a grin.

The contrast was apparent in their work, too. Huston's choice of subjects reflected his interests in sports, the arts, the exotic, and in the kind of excitement that makes life seem like an adventure—or a Huston film. Miller's work inclined more toward the pursuit of meaning than of adventure; he said that drama "is akin to the other inventions of man, in that it ought to help us to know more, and not merely to spend our feelings." One sensed a conflict in him quite different from that in Huston: the rationalist in Miller sometimes seemed at odds with the imagination of the artist. Reason might dismiss some of his most original ideas as crazy and hold back on their deepest pursuit. What would his attitude be toward his wife's albatross? Would he be able to share the burden or persuade her to drop it? She'd never do that; she'd drop him instead.

I had come to talk to them about Monroe's new movie, which was to be filmed in and outside Reno. Nobody could know then it would be her last, but it was a strange coincidence that Huston was to be the director, since he had also directed her at the start of her career in one of her early movies, *The Asphalt Jungle*. He was in at the beginning, and also in at the end in a way that suited Hollywood superstitions. The first time he had directed her, of course, she had been a fledgling; now he was dealing with a star whose approach to acting had become quite different to his. True to his tough-guy image, Huston didn't fuss over his actors, but allowed them a good deal of professional freedom. Monroe believed in a much more introverted, analytical Method approach and, because she was still uncertain of herself in high drama, in which her image wasn't enough, she needed a lot of attention. It was easy to anticipate trouble in Reno.

I felt embarrassed for Miller's sake about the newspaper headlines and tried to keep off the subject of his wife for awhile. How sick he must be of being asked about her instead of about his own work!

Huston talked about the neutral subject of the Irish. In spite of what was said about them, they were really "a modest, very shy people."

"We are so unused to that these days," Miller said, "We are bound to misinterpret it. But I don't think you can stay out of the twentieth century, which is what Ireland seems to be trying to do. . . ."

I began to wonder if he'd seen all those "Marilyn's Husband" headlines. Maybe he had missed them and still had the illusions about Ireland that I'd had.

"Ireland is the reverse of every country in the world," Huston said. "That's why I live here."

There was also the local hunt he enjoyed, the mansion he probably got for a song, compared to American prices, the low income tax. . . . We were still playing roles and I wondered if we'd get beyond them or whether I'd go away empty-handed.

I asked Huston what he looked for in choosing a subject. "Just what interests me," he said, not willing to intellectualize.

"No prerequisites. Not even any standards. Just what gets me."

Miller objected. "It must reflect something of yourself."

Huston replied coolly: "Perhaps in a deeper sense, but not consciously."

Miller said he wouldn't deal with a subject now that he once might have, because it would bore him. "After all, I know more now what I am doing than I did twenty years ago."

Huston didn't agree. "One of the best pictures I ever made was the first—*The Maltese Falcon.*"

They talked about being in and out of fashion, and Huston said: "You get it with painters. Other generations rediscover them. El Greco, Vermeer—they're rediscovered in a time that is similar to their time in some way. And they're neglected in times that have nothing in common with theirs. What would Greco have meant to Victorian England? What would he have meant to those industrialist collectors of the States? Not a damn thing."

Miller said, "There's no doubt that in any art form, there's such a profusion of impulses that people can seize on one and say, 'That's me, that's the way I am.' In a great writer like Shakespeare, there are so many facets, so many things people can latch onto and say: 'This belongs to me,' that there's a Shakespeare in every age. Some facet appeals to every age. Yet there's really only one Shakespeare."

I was to remember this remark about a year later when I learned much more about Miller's wife's many facets. Not only Shakespeare, I thought. I asked Miller why he'd never written a novel after *Focus*. "I don't like the form any more," he told me. "I like plays or movies."

But they required collaboration with others, I said, having in mind the problems that must be ahead for these two very different men in their collaboration on *The Misfits*.

"I don't think it necessarily has to be frustrating," Miller replied. "Though I think it would be after adapting something or after writing cynically. Then it gets boring. There are more movies written cynically than there should be, and perhaps that's why they often seem depleting. There's no reason why a film script should not be valid."

That gave me my opening. "What about *The Misfits*, which Mr. Huston is going to film from your script?"

They looked at each other. At such an early stage of their collaboration, this was delicate. They didn't yet know one another well enough to be sure where the sensitive areas were.

"John, you tell about it," Miller said.

"I wish I could answer that," Huston said carefully, as if it was a State Department briefing and I'd asked some awkward question about Russia. "Well, it's contemporary. It's laid in the West and it's about people who aren't willing to sell their lives."

"That's a good way to put it," Miller said.

"They will sell their work, but they won't sell their lives, and for that reason they're misfits."

"I'm glad we brought this up," Miller said. "Now I know what it's all about. I was once asked what *Death of a Salesman* was about. I tried eighteen different ways. But all I could say was, 'Well, it's about a salesman and he died and after that you're on your own.' "

Huston talked about his approach to the film. You had to find the best way to handle the camera. You could have ideas before you started, but when you were there on location, "that's when it matters. You can find a photographic approach to a film before it starts but not the right camera movement."

He added: "This film we're going to do together, I'll put it on a small screen with no color. It will be the first one for me like that for a long time."

"It will be fun," Miller said, "to get down to business where it belongs—in the middle."

"Of the screen?"

"Yeah. Concentration where it belongs seems to me a sign of a director."

"I think a good writer is a director," Huston said.

They were being extraordinarily polite with each other.

"There's a temperamental thing needed which I haven't got," Miller said.

"Well, I'd be surprised if you *did* have it, Arthur."

"I get tired of being with a lot of people sooner than I should."

"It's different if you're working on it with them," Huston said encouragingly.

"It's this continual observing, John, that's so tiring."

Huston said: "People are always saying to me—novice onlookers—they're surprised how many times a scene may have to be shot, over and over. Well, God, each time you do it, there's a little acceleration of the heartbeat, the pulse. You're praying to Christ nothing happens to spoil it, and then something does, and you have to do it all over again."

This remark must have come back to haunt Huston during the filming of *The Misfits;* some Monroe scenes had to be done twenty times before he thought they were right, particularly the late scenes of high emotion.

"But that's why the medium is so great," Miller said, encouraging Huston in return. My, the two collaborators were certainly trying to meet each other more than half way. "One kind of thing may be spoiled by an accident, but it can also mean spontaneity. Marilyn was doing something in a film scene recently and her hair came down over her face. She figured it was the end of that take. But it looked great. And that's the one they're going to use."

He had mentioned her name first, so I now felt free to do so without seeming to cast him merely as Marilyn's husband and thereby stir depths of resentment. "Is there going to be more scope for Mrs. Miller's talents in your film?"

"Oh, yes, more than anything she's ever done."

I waited for him to go on, but it was dangerous ground. He remained silent, puffing on a cigarette, not wanting to talk any more about it. He wasn't going to play the husband here; he was Arthur Miller.

The two collaborators went on to talk about the difficult problem of telling the truth. A character in Miller's play, *A View from the Bridge*, says that although truth is holy, "most of the time now we settle for half, and I like it better." Miller commented: "I don't share his view, as a matter of fact, but truth can be both admirable and terrible."

Huston said slowly, dramatically, staring in turn at both of us: "I know a story, a tragedy, that reverts back to two people telling each other the truth." He sat forward and fixed his eyes on Miller's as he told slowly, but with perfect timing, the story of a couple who were deeply in love. They had been separated during World War II and when reunited, they asked each other if they had been faithful. "Being two very truthful people, they admitted to each other they had not been faithful." Huston flicked the ash off his cigar. "If they had lied, all might have been well." He laid down the cigar. "As it was, they separated for good."

17

Miller nodded. "Truth destroyed them, unless you take another view, that they had perceived a truth beyond that one."

"Of course," Huston said, "but that was asking too much of them, of their capacities. Truth can be very dangerous."

"Unless you know how to contain it," Miller said.

"Unless you are great enough to handle it," Huston replied.

The essential difference between the two men seemed to come out in this little exchange—Miller seeing safety in intellectual "containment," in reason, while Huston looked for the heroic.

Huston went on to tell another story about the strength that was needed to survive. It concerned a dipsomaniac whose three fine sons seemed unaffected by their father's frequent breakdowns. Miller said he used to work with juvenile delinquents in New York and had often admired youths for surviving destructive influences.

"It's not just environmental," Huston said. "If the personality of the child is strong enough, it can stand an assault from a bad home."

Miller looked thoughtful, and I wondered if he was thinking what I was: that his wife was a good example of a strong personality overcoming a bad start, though she was still very much marked by it. But what he said was: "The forces are too complicated to generalize about."

I asked him if heredity interested him as a writer.

"No," he replied, "I can't make it work in any way, because it's a blank thing to me."

I tried to get back to the theme of *The Misfits*. I recalled that John Steinbeck had recently written about how depressed

18

he was by conditions in the United States when he returned from a long, peaceful stay in an English village.

"I think I know what John meant," Miller said, "but America's always been a materialistic country. It's just that we created that material. Everybody, every country, is like that. There are merely degrees. We've got more of the stuff. And everybody else is trying to get more. Certain things are not valued any longer unless they have some commercial use. Certain codes of behavior can't be converted into money and are going by the board all over the world. People degenerate when they only respond to things because there's a prospect of gain or usefulness. I don't think we're going to get a different code until we reach the point where everything is valueless."

Huston said: "I think one of the troubles is the damned advertising and brainwashing the country takes many times a day."

"Oh, yes, anything goes. Everything always went; it's just that the techniques have become so good."

"It's not just in America," Huston said. "It's going to be everywhere. It doesn't do a country any good."

"It doesn't do anybody any good unless you can be immune," Miller said. "The argument in favor of doing things is that it's profitable. That's its justification. Somebody's got to say that things which are profitable are not necessarily right. Just to make that statement would be treasonous."

I asked if the movie would deal with this topic.

"No, but it's in the air now, all right," Miller said. "An extraordinary number of people are conscious of the dead end it represents. There's a radio station outside New York City, on Long Island, that has no advertising at all and it survives by providing good programs—jazz, classical music, discussions between artists, serious programs like that. People were asked if they would send twelve dollars a year to support the station. And do you know, it's doing great."

"That's very hopeful," Huston said.

"I only learned about it last week when I was over at my brother's house, and he said a lot of people were sending in their twelve dollars. You don't become a vice-president for that or get on the board; you just get a receipt."

"Why twelve dollars?" Huston asked.

"I don't know. It's an odd number. Perhaps it's like in the stores asking for $6.98 instead of seven dollars. It's a purely voluntary thing. But it's encouraging."

Huston got up on his crutches and went off for a few minutes. In his absence Miller talked about Huston's young son who had recently caught a giant salmon. "It broke the fishing net," he said admiringly and showed me the remains of the net, spreading it out with his large, workmanlike hands. He looked out the window at the Huston estate. "The boy's out there fishing now," he said enviously.

Glimpsing a horse in the distance, I asked Miller if he was going to do any riding in Ireland to prepare for the rodeo world of *The Misfits*.

"Did you say riding or writing? I'm not going to do any riding, particularly after what happened to John. But I'm always writing."

Both men came to the great door of the mansion to see me off. I had the feeling that there was a third person between them, for Monroe had haunted the conversation for me even though there had been few references to her. Would Miller's visit pave the way for the difficult Huston-Monroe collaboration to come? Or would he completely reject the role of Marilyn's husband? Huston wasn't the kind of man to have much sympathy for a husband playing second fiddle.

"See you in Reno," I told them.

Huston gave his actor's smile; Miller looked impassive.

I remembered the newspaper headlines. More than ever, they seemed degrading—of her as well as him. And of us, too.

I didn't want to follow *The Misfits* from the beginning because I had had enough experience of movie work to know that nobody would have time to talk to an outsider until relationships had been established and some progress had been made. I planned to reach Reno after the Huston-Miller partnership had been tested and the danger of its developing into a contest was over. By then Marilyn Monroe would have finished with her image publicity and might be prepared to talk. There had to be a real person behind the dumb-blonde gossip items. But if she didn't want to reveal anything of herself, there was always Clark Gable, the old king of Hollywood, who was playing opposite her. I was determined not to become obsessed with Monroe, as so many journalists had.

The Misfits, I had discovered, was based on an old Miller short story about three drifting cowboys who force mustangs out of the mountains with a low-flying airplane and sell the meat. Miller had said all his work dealt with "what is in the air"; how did *The Misfits* deal with people's current preoccupations?

On the way to Reno I decided to sample what was "in the air" and get some experience of real cowboys at the famous Pendleton rodeo in Oregon. The visit soon taught me once again to admire the form, meaning, and harmony that art finds in the chaos of life. Nothing I saw at Pendleton was about anything except exercising a skill for money. The indifference to the feelings of the animals involved was extraordinary. I might as well have tried to find meaningful symbols for our time in a game of professional tennis. The cowboys didn't seem like misfits in the present any more than the noncowboy residents of the town. Pendleton was out of the fashionable eastern mainstream represented by New York and Washington, D.C. but it was still contemporary Americana.

The most successful cowboys flew from rodeo to rodeo in their private planes. The younger, less successful ones, who traveled by Greyhound bus like me, seemed more interested in the latest pop tunes than anything as heady as old-fashioned independence in the Huston-Miller sense. Their overheard conversation, like that of people on the streets of New York, was always about money. They certainly didn't sound like free souls "willing to sell their work but not their lives." From their talk they seemed willing to sell *anything* if the price was right.

I went to a businessman's cocktail party. Instead of hearing the usual golf talk of big-city parties, I listened to tales of hunts in the hills—real safaris seemingly the way they told it. Guns were as much a part of life as cigarettes; sophistication seemed to stop there. It was an election year, but talk about Vice-President Nixon versus Senator Kennedy was on a fairly simple level.

Most of the cowboys I talked with seemed to be very conservative. They referred with deadpan respect to the "Vice-President." Patriotism seemed to be an excuse not to think; they were against the remotest change in the status quo. Most of them had never heard of Huston or Miller, but they all knew of Marilyn Monroe, and some felt bound to make sex jokes about her—the kind of jokes that make the teller sound insecure. I didn't want to see a full-length movie about these characters and hoped that Miller had chosen a less conformist bunch or had transformed them into the intense beings of real

26

art and not just romanticized them. Otherwise the collaboration would be under great strain from the beginning—and so would the actors.

Rumors were already trickling into the newspapers about the early days on location. The Monroe-Miller marriage was said to be on the rocks. Monroe was reported to be in love with the star of her last movie, the French actor, Yves Montand. I never took movie gossip seriously. Imaginations generally ran wild out of boredom, but so much gossip so early was a bad sign. I took a Greyhound bus down the coast, through the mighty redwoods, planning to reach Reno by way of San Francisco but without losing too much time.

I wanted to see the first Nixon-Kennedy TV debate and stopped off at a seedy-looking motel along the way. But the TV there had broken down and the newest set was in a bar on the other side of a bridge. Unfortunately, the bridge had room for cars but none for pedestrians. Presumably pedestrians were out-of-date, misfits in California's mechanistic society, in which one of the big local hobbies was racing aimlessly up and down the superhighways.

Ten minutes before the debate was due to begin, I tried running across the dimly lit bridge and nearly didn't make it. Motorists either didn't see me until the last minute or enjoyed giving the impression that they were going to run me down. I didn't enjoy the debate—both Nixon and Kennedy appeared incredibly tense—but I got more of an impression of what might be in the air. Whereas Nixon stood on Eisenhower's shoulders, defending the status quo of the past eight years, Kennedy tried to convince people that the country needed a change, to move on. An attack on conformity and complacency was implied. Were there enough misfits to agree with him? My interest in the answer was affected by the nagging thought that

27

I had to make it back across the bridge, so I didn't give the two candidates my full attention.

When I had dinner with a wealthy couple in San Francisco the next night (people I had met in Oregon asked me to call on them), the hostess inquired about my reaction to the debate and what my choice would be in the election. I said I wasn't very impressed by either of the presidential candidates, but I much preferred Kennedy to Nixon. The woman amazed me by becoming hysterically abusive, which was then unique in my experience of hostesses. They are usually more tolerant of eccentric guests. She seemed to regard Kennedy as a Red. Her outburst made the cowboys in Miller's story seem thoroughly contemporary; this woman was about as ignorant of twentieth-century realities as her ancestors, wherever they came from. I was supposed to stay the night, but I fled. Reporters had to get in training like boxers, but surely the cowboys, and Nixon and Kennedy, and now this, had prepared me for Miller's misfits, and I decided to make Reno without any further delay.

The latest news from the front line (they were filming on a dry lake outside Reno) was that work on the movie had been stopped while Monroe went in a hospital and recuperated for a few days, but she was now back at work. It sounded bad. Maybe she had found out that she was a misfit among the misfits. She began to seem more interesting.

4

Everyone had reached the dangerous stage of boredom, not only with themselves, but with each other. Reno is supposed to be a fun city that will take away your boredom, but everyone on *The Misfits* had "done" Reno, just as they had exhausted the possibilities of each other. They were like a Swiss Family Robinson that had been through too much together; all they wanted now was to separate and go home. But that was a long way off yet. As a diversion, therefore, people were intensifying their political games and taking sides. If you were pro-Marilyn, you were said to be anti-Arthur; if you were pro-Huston, you were anti-Paula Strasberg, Marilyn's drama coach; and so on.

Rumors circulated as freely as in Washington, D.C. There was a whole collection about Marilyn and her drug problems. The film unit's doctor, a tough, no-nonsense frontier type, was said to be critical of her doctors for allowing her a regular supply of pills. He himself had refused her any more. Before work was stopped for a few days, she was supposed to have been so much under the influence that not only was she hours late for work each day, but some members of her entourage had to walk her round and round her bedroom before she was ready to go. She was said to be barely on speaking terms with Miller, though they were trying to keep up appearances in spite of several public snubs administered by Marilyn in a bad mood. God only knew what was true and what was false in the rumors, but they certainly built up a great feeling of anticipation to see the star of all these stories.

31

When I walked around Reno and saw the lone husbands and lone wives waiting for divorces—as Miller had once done before he married Marilyn—I wondered if the Millers' breakup had been accelerated by the atmosphere. It wasn't easy to believe in romantic love in Reno; nearly 5,000 divorces had been granted there the previous year. You could see the ex-wives emerge from the legal offices and courtrooms and toss their wedding rings into the Truckee River, like prisoners losing their chains. Adultery, cruelty, desertion, alcoholism, non-support: the reasons for ending the marriages were ticked off as unemotionally as the Dow-Jones average. If the gamblers in the casinos seemed to work by automation, so did the divorcing couples. You could see them, these disenchanted people, at all times of the day or night, whiling away the six weeks they had to be there to qualify for a divorce: perched over cards, spinning wheels or working the one-armed bandits. Many of them were people who would never have thought of gambling at home, wherever that was. They got in the way of the real gamblers who sometimes had only a weekend in which to make their fortune—or sell their shirts at a pawnshop for a bus ticket back to where they came from. The combination of divorce and gambling would have depressed a booming optimist; it was a desperate background for a woman who had to live on pills and whose marriage was said to be breaking up. I waited impatiently to see how she looked after all these hard weeks. Where the hell was she?

All the journalists had come and gone, so I was welcomed as a new face. The publicity people gave me a copy of the script to read as if it were a top-secret document. Arthur, I was told, was still rewriting every night. One of his problems was that he couldn't get the ending right: who won Monroe in the end? Perhaps he found the answer so hard because he felt her slipping away from him. The Monroe role hadn't been in the original short story; Miller, however, had written the script around a new character, a woman who was picked up by the cowboys. Much of the suspense came from wondering which of the cowboys would finally get her. In the version I was given, the older cowboy, played by Clark Gable, won her, but there was said to be another ending that awarded her to the younger, wilder cowboy played by Montgomery Clift. Miller was still working on it. I wondered which cowboy he identified with. Whoever it was would probably get Marilyn in the end. My money was on Gable.

I met the producer, Frank Taylor, a former New York book editor and a friend of Miller's. A tall, slim, elegant man, he spoke quietly, unlike many Hollywood producers. He listened, too, which was even more unlike the breed. A general peacemaker among the various groups, Taylor acted as a buffer between Huston and Miller and the Hollywood Studio executives and backers.

I told Taylor that I'd like to talk with Miller and Huston, to catch up on the progress of their collaboration since Ireland. He was a little evasive, and I caught a glimpse of the huge worries hidden by his bland manner. He said Miller was devoting *all* his time to rewriting. While we were talking—we were in a hotel bar—Huston came in. He seemed remote, as if his thoughts were back home in Galway. He was no longer on crutches, but he looked even paler, thinner, and more somber. Someone told me later that he had just gambled and lost an enormous sum. At least he wouldn't have to sell his shirt at a pawnshop. I wondered how much the strain of collaboration and the Monroe breakdown had contributed to his gloom but decided to leave that until later.

I asked Taylor about Monroe. Was she available? Now he

was even more evasive. He could promise nothing. I had better ask the publicity people. They could speak to her secretary, May Reis. The answer soon came back: nothing doing; Monroe wasn't giving interviews. I assumed she was in too bad a shape. Well, I wasn't heartbroken. I wouldn't lose my job on the *Manchester Guardian* if I never talked to her, and it would leave me free to write about the making of *The Misfits* as a whole, rather than concentrating on the star.

Huston must have regretted his remoteness, because next morning I was invited to drive to the location with him. He showed no sign of gambler's depression and talked ironically about the presidential campaign, summing it up in one line: "Who do they think we are?"

The dark sky made an early start on the day's work impossible, so Huston stopped at the Nevada State Museum in Carson City to look at the Indian section and perhaps stimulate his imagination for the day's work. As he peered into the glass cases devoted to Indian tribes, his long, lean head and figure more than ever resembled a totem pole. Up the road, where he next chose to stop, was an antique store specializing in mementoes of the old West. A black cat that met him at the door was greeted in the way that only a bigtime gambler can greet such a token of future fortune. But after taking a quick, knowledgeable look at the children's toys, furniture, and guns of the last century, Huston strode back to his car empty-handed and pronounced himself ready for the weather reports from the dry lake about fifty miles from Reno, where the day's scenes were to be shot.

The weather scouts reported back to the small town of Dayton. As Huston's car drove up in a cloud of dust, Clark Gable came over. He was still burly, but without some of the bursting energy he had once conveyed. Now he was dressed as

34

a cowboy but was smoking from a long, sophisticated cigarette holder. He told us about a tame bobcat kept by a family in the town.

This seemed to console Huston after the gloomy weather news. No work would be possible that day, and he went off to see the bobcat for himself. A famous nonconformist in the conformist film industry, he was fascinated by the taming of any wild animal. It was easier now to see why the story of *The Misfits* had attracted him. The cowboys were threatened with the same fate as the bobcat.

While I was talking to Gable—whose famous wicked grin concealed a simple, direct man, more like a thoroughly professional stage actor than a big movie star—I noticed a woman in sloppy pants with a faded scarf tied around her hair. I thought she was a local housewife come to ogle the movie stars until I saw that she was with Arthur Miller (a much more gaunt and wearier Miller than the man I'd met in Ireland). Then I realized who she was. I had been waiting for a grand entrance as shiningly beautiful as her photographs—or perhaps the shattered appearance of a woman on the rocks. Anyway, something dramatic and memorable. I had been fooled by the image. I caught only a glimpse of the famous face—it didn't look famous, but neither did it look broken up—before she and Miller were following Huston to see the bob-cat. From the back they looked like an ordinary couple hardly worth a second glance. Perhaps the most memorable thing about them was that they were together. Perhaps all the rumors about a separation were untrue. I wondered if this was one of those cases Huston had talked about in Ireland, where it was better not to know the truth.

5

The next day the weather showed an improvement, though it was still far from the heat wave of a few weeks—and scenes —before, when it had touched 106 degrees. Under a pale, blue-white sky with a few chunks of dark cloud, Huston completed a scene after twenty-three takes. He was ready to begin another when a slight breeze whipped up the sand on the dry lake and the sun slid behind one of the bigger clouds. Huston threw away a half-smoked cigar in disgust, Miller puffed thoughtfully on his pipe, and Monroe drained a glass of water hastily brought by one of her entourage. After all these weeks in the dry Nevada desert, she had a dry cough, like everyone else.

I arranged to have a meeting with Miller and also with Montgomery Clift. I chatted some more with Clark Gable. But I left Monroe and her entourage alone. I noticed her watching me curiously as I talked to Gable. Rumor had it that Gable, who always arrived on time and liked to leave on time, had become so infuriated with her lateness that he had shut himself in his trailer until she apologized. When she at last drove up, the story went, Huston sent everybody away and persuaded her to knock on Gable's trailer door and say she was sorry.

I would have liked to know whether it was true, but Gable, when I asked him, just gave his famous chuckle. Huston was busy that day, and Monroe was unreachable. I didn't feel like asking Miller, and that left my question open only to the rumormongers who swore that it was accurate. In time it didn't seem to matter. The atmosphere wasn't created so much by what happened as by what people thought had happened.

This time it was the weather, not Monroe, that was causing the delay. For a few minutes, everyone sat waiting impatiently, like a group of ancient sun-worshippers, but when the sun showed no sign of reappearing they all resigned themselves and formed two baseball teams captained by Miller and Huston—the collaborators in competition!—with Huston's team batting first. At the first big hit there was the whine of a police siren and the two resident policemen in their patrol car roared across the desert in pursuit of the ball. It was a touch worthy of Huston himself. The Miller Yankees, with their long-legged captain looking comparatively professional in a golfing cap, were beginning to get the better of the Huston Giants when out came the sun. Play was abruptly abandoned, and *The Misfits* began to roll again.

Huston was filming it the way he had said he would back in Galway—concentrating on the characters. Since the advent of the wide screen, the tendency in Hollywood, particularly in westerns, had been to let the landscape come to the foreground and dominate the picture, dwarfing the people in it. This may be desirable with most Hollywood scripts, which reduce the people to mere types anyway, but *The Misfits* had real characters—human bobcats—and Huston wanted to make the most of them. Such unusual concentration put added strain on the actors, a deadly strain for most film actors, for they have little or no acting technique and generally need all the scenic and other diversions they can get to distract the keen-eyed from their histrionic shortcomings. But Huston had a group of professionals and was helping them all he could by filming *The Misfits* in continuity, which meant starting at the beginning and finishing at the end. Usually scenes were filmed in the order that most helped the budget. The poor actors might play the end today and the beginning tomorrow, making a logical development of character impossible for the average player. Both Gable and Monroe had to show a complicated emotional switch in a subtle relationship, and Huston's method of filming, although perhaps more costly, was a great help to them. The black-and-white film devotedly studying the quartet's every change of mood had the look of an etching, which no doubt was one of Huston's aims, for he often tried to match the effects of some of his favorite artists.

I could see this clearly as I watched him composing a picture around the wild horses that had been caught especially for him. No painter could have grouped them with a keener eye for balance and composition. In the frame he arranged the horses with Gable, Clift, and Eli Wallach in the foreground and with Monroe watching them with horror in the background. Arthur Miller, a lonely figure on the fringe of the desert, brooding over some aspect of the script, looked suddenly worried as the group came to life, and he hurried over to consult one of the cowboys—a real cowboy looking after the wild horses—about "whether Marilyn would be in any danger if the horses went forward instead of back." The cowboy assured him that the horses were trained to be obedient from the front and to kick up at the rear—"They're professional actors!" Miller grinned and went back to his brooding, leaving Huston, who was finally satisfied with his grouping, to finish the scene. "Action!" cried Huston with an ironical grin.

"Mr. Miller knows a lot about horses," volunteered one of the cowboys, and another—permanently employed on Hollywood westerns ("Just done *The Alamo* with John Wayne, and they want me on the new John Ford picture.")—said the film was one of the most authentic he had ever worked on.

41

"Mr. Huston won't stand for any faking." Certainly the professional cowboys could never have had it so good if status was what appealed to them. Man-of-action Huston consulted them about the finer points of cowboy life with near reverence, and a veteran member of the unit confided: "John would rather have been a real cowboy than President."

But the picture that kept coming back to me was of Miller so worried about his wife's safety that he checked with one of the cowboys about it. Surely the rumors had to be wrong. I nearly bumped into her when we were both leaving the dry lake to go back to the hotel. Considering all she was supposed to have been through in the last few weeks, she looked wonderful. She stared at me as if she was about to speak, but I hurried on, remembering her rejection of my request for an interview. I had an appointment with Montgomery Clift in a hotel bar and I was already late.

Montgomery Clift was even later. He arrived at last as if he was walking on air, a fixed grin turning this way and that, as if he had forgotten what I looked like. I waved and he came over—a small, thin man with a shy lope, his face, once as delicate and striking as a pretty girl's, now hurt looking, the result not only of a bad accident a few years ago but of living without adequate spiritual protection. He always gave me the impression of someone who wanted to cry but had decided to try to laugh it off. He approached me now like a shy animal on stiff legs, his grin still fixed and rather vacant-looking. He mumbled something that might have been in a foreign language for all the sense it made to me. I asked him to repeat it. He did so, much louder, grinning all the time, but still it made no sense. I realized then that he was so drunk, he was incoherent. He stopped and shrugged as if to say he had done his best and there was nothing else he could do. I didn't know

42

what to say. He had an intense lyrical style as an actor that I admired a great deal. Friends said he couldn't handle his homosexuality, and the bad car accident that cut up his face had led to heavy drinking. So I was prepared in a way to find him like this and I was sympathetic. We stood staring at each other, both speechless. Eventually a publicity man led him away as if he was a powerless little boy.

Next day on the dry lake, looking pale and nervous, he apologized and said to tell him anytime I wanted to talk and we could have a session in his room and play some records. I tried to convey that it hadn't mattered a damn and also, without actually saying so, that of course I wouldn't write about it in my newspaper. He had some right to get drunk. I suspected his performances were so good because he was such an open man and that is a very painful way to be.

I noticed Monroe watching us talk. She and Montgomery Clift were supposed to be very close. She looked puzzled, and I wondered what she was thinking. Maybe she was just worried that I might take a hard line with him. She went on watching us like a concerned mother hen.

As if deliberately stimulating their imaginations, many of *The Misfits* spent much of their free time in Virginia City, one of the most famous ghost towns in the West. Miller and Monroe were there and so were Huston and Gable and Clift. The ghost town, an offspring of the gold rush, had rarely seen such activity since it was left behind by the twentieth century.

Such remains of the old West are as meaningful for Americans as Roman relics are for Europeans. It was their exact meaning for us today that Arthur Miller was after in *The Misfits*. Like an archaeologist on a prolonged dig, he had worked for three years at the task of sifting Western remains, measuring the few real cowboys who were still, in spite of all the twentieth-century temptations, doggedly loyal to the old life represented by the ghost towns. He had tried to do for the modern cowboy what Hemingway once did for the bullfighter, and that was to blow away Hollywood's romantic smokescreens and put the man into true perspective. Typical of Miller's separation of the real and the false in Western life today was his description of a group at a rodeo: "There are cowboys in working clothes, and many in the tight shirts and jeans they saw in the movies."

Miller had lived in a cottage at Pyramid Lake when he came for his divorce several years before, and had visited Reno only occasionally, usually to pick up his laundry. "I didn't look around much," he told me. "Nothing seemed to make much of an impression." Yet Reno became the spiritual center of his

47

story, underlining, with its divorce and gambling scenes of disenchantment, the hard struggle of the principal characters to find a meaningful relationship. "It was probably helpful that I didn't get to see too much," he now decided. "If I had, I might have got lost in the detail. As it was, just seeing Reno an hour at a time made it always seem startling. Now I've been here for months and I never even look twice at the casinos, at the gambling that would be illegal where I come from but here is an accepted part of everyday life."

Did one catch glimpses of Miller's view of his wife in the character of Roslyn? A friend tells her, "Cowboys are the last real men in the world, but they're as reliable as jackrabbits," and she muses: "Is anybody any different? Maybe you aren't supposed to believe what people say. Maybe it's not even fair to them." Roslyn is a kind of Mary Magdalen figure who has survived the worst of the world, and she tells the three cowboys: "You know everything except what it feels like to be alive. You're three dear, sweet, dead men."

At night Miller rewrote the script and then he and Huston would have a conference to discuss the new lines. "What do you think of this, John?"

"Read it again, kid," Huston was in charge now; Miller was on the defensive.

The strain on Miller was beginning to tell. He said one night that he wouldn't work on another film for "a long, long time." Yet on location the next day, he was relaxed enough to go in a store in Dayton, a town of about 200 people, for ice cream and chat easily with the owner. Why had she settled in Dayton? Well, she and her husband had been going to Reno when they saw Dayton and they liked the willow trees there, so they stopped. "She liked the willow trees," said Miller wonderingly, inspecting the lofty trees that partly ringed the store.

48

I asked him about the ending of *The Misfits*, which seemed more optimistic than the conclusions of his plays. Had he changed? "There is a change," he said. "For a long time now I've wanted to make something of existence. It's tragic—after all, we all die here—but there's something in between. Gay and Roslyn will die, but they can face it with dignity. They can do right, and not be like the jerks. It may not sound much but it's taken a lot to get me to that point." He put down his pipe and munched a plum. "I feel a failure with all my writing. I never seem to get down on paper the effect it has had on me. That's why in this film it's been very difficult when John or the actors have come and questioned a line, not to think they are bound to be right. I've had to learn that maybe I'm right and they're blaming my lines for something they should do themselves."

When he eventually went off to bed, he planned to get up at 3:00 A.M. for the final rewriting of the scene between Roslyn and Gay before leaving for the location about nine. There wasn't much time for sleep.

It was rare now to see him with Monroe. They seldom talked together. Rumor had it that he had secretly moved into another room in the hotel and left her for good.

I had the impression that Huston had drawn a professional veil between him and everyone else. His aim was to get the movie completed before any more disasters occurred. It was like standing in a mine field among all those manic-depressive people. Huston himself couldn't afford to explode. His escape had to come in gambling, in rather mean practical jokes, or in the sense of manipulating everyone else. I watched him look sourly at Paula Strasberg as she talked intensely to Marilyn Monroe between takes. *How many damned directors are there on this movie?* his expression seemed to say, but he didn't say anything. His tough-guy charm generally made women easy to handle, but Monroe had gone off on her own into a great remoteness. There was surface friendliness; Huston often addressed her as "honey." But I sensed that both of them had withdrawn from the other. And Miller stood uneasily between them.

It is a writer's burden that he is vulnerable to a director. The collaboration had had no chance at equality from the start. Miller looked more and more tired. It was hard, too, on the script girl, Angela Allen. She had to do all the hasty retyping. At the height of the rumors about her and Montand, Monroe had retaliated by speaking meanly of Angela and Miller, as if they were having an affair. Angela resented it; and Monroe was not popular with her. Publicity always made much of Monroe's childhood among foster parents and rapists, and Angela commented: "Other people had hard childhoods, but they got over it." Monroe certainly never did, perhaps because she was continually being reminded of it. Yet if her childhood had been half as bad with a succession of strangers as her publicity claimed, it was a wonder she had survived at all.

She seemed to be living her role this time. The high nervous emotion she expressed in the later scenes of *The Misfits* seemed to have been rehearsed in her breakdown, when work had stopped, and in her outbursts at Miller. She worried her way into a scene, into re-creating an emotion. Take after take was needed until she was ragged enough to live the scene. It was an approach that was very hard on her, her director, and her fellow actors, and everyone looked for the early signs of another breakdown. Frank Taylor knew they were already well over the budget and that the backers in Hollywood were worried.

One morning on the dry lake I watched her repeat an emotional outburst ten times before Huston was satisfied with her nuances, with the other actors, with the composition of the scene as a whole—with the hundred and one details which make a Huston effect. Again and again, at Huston's jovial bidding ("Okay, try it again, honey"), she would begin screaming "Murderers!" at Gable, Clift, and Wallach, jumping in and out of a state of high emotion without any preparatory passages in a way a stage actor need never do.

The wear and tear on the nerves must have been savage. Paula Strasberg whispered encouragement between each repeat while someone else gave her large spoonfuls of some vitamin-laden liquid. She sat grimly waiting, like a boxer in his corner trying to warm up so that he will be ready to fight immediately at his best when the bell sounds. At the end she looked pale and exhausted, and the entourage all but carried her away.

I was surprised then in the early afternoon to see her looking composed and dazzling in a simple dress—looking, in fact, every inch her image. She was so clever at makeup that one was never sure what she was masking, but her powers of recuperation, at least over a short period, were also very strong. She was out shopping with Eddie Parone, the young New York theater director who was Frank Taylor's assistant producer. I heard her say to him: "Who's that?" He told her and she asked to be introduced. She gave me a friendly smile and said coyly: "I've seen you talk to everyone but me."

I felt as if I were supposed to roll over on my back like a dog and howl. I still had some of my prejudice against Arthur's wife for turning him into "Marilyn's husband," and I said offhandedly that I'd been told that she didn't want to be bothered.

"Who said that?"

"I asked for an interview and I was told you weren't giving any." I was too canny to name any culprits.

"Well, how about a drink?" she said with a smile and invited me to meet her in the hotel bar in a couple of hours. I expected the drain of the repeated performances would have depressed her (she was usually ill toward the end of all her movies) and that talking would be difficult, but that was not so.

She entered the dimly lit hotel bar in a girlish flutter that suggested shyness at meeting a stranger—was this a role she had given herself?—and began to relax only when we found a common liking for dimly lit surroundings. There were some rather hearty golfers in the bar, and she confided that she had played golf with a former husband—"I was quite good at it as well, at least I could hit all right, but I never liked the things

55

that went with it." I heartily agreed, and finding this much in common, too, she relaxed a little more.

Wishing to draw her out on *The Misfits*, I remarked on Roslyn's achievement at not being hard-boiled in spite of some harsh experiences. I had in mind Monroe's own experiences, too. "Oh," she murmured in that soft girlish voice, "but don't you find all people who have suffered are like that? They remain nice and sensitive. They do." She laughed a little self-consciously at her own insistence. Perhaps she was thinking of having posed for those seedy nude calendars, the struggle to get bit roles in films, the rigid typing of her as a dumb blonde when she showed some talent. Hollywood had destroyed more talent by typing it than could be counted, and her successful escape seemed an astounding achievement to anyone familiar with the film industry.

When I referred to this, it reminded her of Betty Grable, who had graced many undistinguished Hollywood musicals in the forties and who was marketed as a sex symbol. Upon hearing Grable thus described, Miss Monroe dropped her friendly manner and reared back, saying firmly that she had great respect for *Miss* Grable. "I remember somebody telling me how much her films meant to people in the Pacific during the war. She *helped* them." But wasn't hers a very minor talent? "How do we know what she might have done if she had had the chance? She got typed." Miss Monroe uttered the word *typed* as if it meant being imprisoned. "But she might have done anything if she had been freer. I have great respect for her."

She told me a story about being taken into Betty Grable's dressing room to be introduced and how she suddenly realized that this was the studio's crude way of conveying to Betty Grable that her reign was over and here was her successor. "They tried to take me into her dressing room as if I were

56

taking over. I couldn't do that." She had marched out in disgust, but the incident obviously still haunted her. She saw it happening one day to herself and she had determined to be gone long before then, into the theater or character acting. She admired Betty Grable as someone who had helped to make her own career possible: she saw herself not as the unique sex symbol of her publicity, but as part of a tradition. She was determined, however, never to be typed again the way Betty Grable was. "I'll never tie myself to a studio again. I would rather retire."

Talk of Betty Grable turned to old movies. I was enthusiastic about Michael Chekhov's performance as the old psychiatrist in Hitchcock's *Spellbound* as an example of fine character acting. I didn't know that the great Russian actor had been one of her first teachers until she mentioned it. "Then he died," she said with the lost air of a little girl. In a Miller short story entitled "Please Don't Kill Anything," the heroine, who was obviously based on Monroe, is described this way: "Now she looked up at him like a little girl, with that naked wonder in her face even as she was smiling in the way of a grown woman." It seemed to describe exactly the paradox of Marilyn Monroe that afternoon. Suddenly shy, she told how in class she had once played Cordelia to Chekhov's King Lear. "He gave the greatest performance I have ever seen. It was so wonderful." She gripped my hand impulsively. "You must go and tell Mrs. Chekhov what you told me about *Spellbound*. Now Mr. Chekhov is dead, she so seldom hears people mention him. The public in America is so fickle. She lives in Los Angeles. I'll give you her address and phone number."

Mention of her performance as Cordelia led me to ask her if she wanted to play more Shakespeare. Her shyness increased. Well, she would like to—one day. "I don't like to talk about

57

it, but in a long, long time I would like to play Lady MacBeth."
She paused as if fearing that I might find her wish amusing—
as some journalists had. Reassured, she added: "And it would
be marvelous if MacBeth could be Marlon Brando." She suddenly raced on, her interest in the subject overcoming her
embarrassment: "I have done a few scenes at the Actors Studio. I did a French play. I adapted it a little to make it modern.
I'll give you a copy if you like."

Not only a Shakespearean actress but an adapter as well.
She obviously intended to leave the dumb-blonde image as far
behind as possible. The impression she made at that moment
was a touching one: a beautiful woman, lauded for her good
looks, who had belatedly discovered that she had talent as well
and was trying to plumb it to discover how best to develop
herself. In doing so, she showed an uneasiness about her lack
of formal education. In the last few years she had made rapid
progress in educating herself about so much she felt was
beyond her, but obviously her feeling of insecurity about this
still ran deep. For all her nonconformity and unblunted instincts, she had the American hang-up about going to college.
She made a breathless reference to Bernard Shaw—stressing
the second syllable in *Bernard* in a way that would have
charmed Shaw—and then excused herself with a shy "Of
course, I have no education. I have a lot to catch up." I wanted
to say that she had had a great deal of education, to argue with
her about experience as education, but I thought it better not
to get into that. It was our first meeting and I was only an
interviewer. It was a sore point with her: *leave it alone.*

Arthur Miller came into the bar and told her he was going
to another conference with Huston. They seemed quite
friendly with each other: maybe the rumors were wrong. They
surely wouldn't have done that for the sake of appearances.

58

Miller looked haggard and envious of our having a good time. I wished she'd smile at him, but he went off abruptly without any encouragement.

We were joined by secretary May Reis and Ralph Roberts, Marilyn's masseur. May Reis was a small, mild woman, respected for her loyalty to liberal causes even when they were lost causes. Ralph Roberts was a big, broad, slow-moving, gentle man. Obviously they both increased Marilyn Monroe's feeling of security. She sat back and talked more easily.

We chatted about her approach to a role, and she grew suddenly uneasy in talking about it, as if afraid of trying to catch something that was partly instinctive. "You find out what she's like—the person you're playing. I mean, what she *means* to you. How you're like her and not like her."

I referred to the scene I had watched her play that morning as a big scene and she quickly corrected me, though with a smile, so I wouldn't be offended: "There are no big scenes. They're all equally important—if you have a good director. And if you haven't, nothing is going to matter anyway."

The conversation veered off again into acting techniques, and she mentioned Mr. Chekhov's exercises for developing the voice and the imagination. All of us were relaxed by this time. When she talked about the English actor, John Gielgud, and how much she admired him, I said I thought his technique was admirable, but there was a withdrawn quality about him. He couldn't express the animal emotion needed for some of the great roles. Marilyn Monroe, gaily hanging onto the phrase, "animal emotion," thought his animal emotion was only waiting to be released and suggested a film of Somerset Maugham's *Rain*, with herself as the prostitute, Sadie Thompson, and John Gielgud as the introverted, repressed minister who eventually erupts with passion. "I'm sure his animal emotion would come out then," she said. "Aren't a lot of men like that—all shut up and then suddenly they explode?" She looked at me as if I might be included in that category. "Why don't you write it for me?" she said in her most alluring manner.

Ah, until she said that, she had nearly won me over. I had come to see her almost as simple and charming as the girl next door. But now she was trying to woo me, to win over yet another journalist, another interviewer. I had been through that experience before with movie stars and politicians, and she began to lose me.

Back, then, to strict business and the role of Roslyn, though she clearly didn't want to analyze it. Was she beginning to tire of Roslyn, of that starry-eyed view of her? "She's only a girl I play, a girl who knows what life can be and therefore responds to it." She was just starting to develop her thoughts about Roslyn, the way she saw her role, when a man at a nearby table crushed a moth. She stopped what she was saying and watched him in consternation as if wanting to cry "Stop!" It was painful to see her. I remembered what Miller had written in "Please Don't Kill Anything": "While part of his heart worshipped her fierce tenderness toward all that lived, another part knew that she must come to understand that she did not die with the moths and the spiders and the fledgling birds. . . ."

Each day after work she and each member of her entourage put a silver dollar on a table in the casino that occupied the lobby of the hotel, and that day she included me when she handed out the coins. Nobody had any luck. When I, the last one, put my dollar down she clapped her hands and cried, "Oh, I do hope he wins," and watched the wheel spin it away. "Oh, I'm so sorry," she said with a quick surge of sympathy and

60

invited me up to her suite for a salami sandwich as if to make up for any lingering disappointment.

The perfect hostess, she took me out onto the balcony to see the river in the starlight and pointed out where the ducks might be seen during the day. Passing a large wall mirror, she stopped, went back, and seemed strangely disappointed. "My nose looks kinda shiny," she said with a grimace.

A deliveryman brought a sheaf of color publicity photographs for her to approve, and she rejected them all. The deliveryman looked very unhappy. What an odd combination of seasoned star and little girl she seemed then between the photographs and the ducks. Arthur Miller had said once that only the French really appreciated his wife, that the Americans were too puritanical to realize that a beautiful woman, a sex symbol, could also possess talent and intelligence. Perhaps this puritanism lay at the back of the obstinate attempts to type her. The next day, May Reis showed me an item written by a Californian columnist which implied that she had a vocabulary of about a hundred words and that in signing a visitor's book somewhere, she had had to ask how to spell "marvelous." Once cast as a dumb blonde, always a dumb blonde for some people. The entourage was seething.

Yet witness her eagerly awaited arrival on the set, perhaps a little late, or more than a little—which was an annoyance to her fellow professionals, though they were usually understanding enough to attribute it to a delicate temperament. She was the queen bee in the middle of her modest retinue, and you might have expected to see one of the old-time great actresses of the stage come sweeping in—one like Mrs. Patrick Campbell who could subdue even Bernard Shaw. Instead, you found a beautiful blonde with a shy, yet whimsical, manner, a touch of Mrs. Patrick Campbell's star authority, and a touch of Shirley Temple.

To my surprise, I liked Arthur's wife. She wasn't what I had expected; she was certainly much more complex. I wondered to what extent I was falling before the assault of a professional beauty, a skilled charmer. Not that she could have cared what I personally thought of her, but I represented a newspaper which she—and Miller—respected: it may have been a matter of professional pride to have an approving article published there. Yet there was something indefinably shy about her, an almost old-fashioned inferiority complex and fear of rejection, a wallflower streak in the beautiful woman. But it was too much to think that she feared rejection by me, one of a thousand journalists who flocked to her, after all her years of fame. I still thought I had much more in common with Miller than with her, and I hardened my heart. I detested journalists who ass-kissed the famous and powerful, particularly those who allowed themselves to be used by politicians. Not having fallen for Eisenhower's charm, I was determined not to succumb to Marilyn Monroe's.

But our meeting had certainly broken a barrier and gotten me accepted by her entourage. Next morning I received a beaming smile from them all; Marilyn even waved. The anti-Marilyn groups looked me over and began to reassess me. One of the photographers who was sour about it asked me how I had managed it, as if I had won an exclusive interview by some professional con-man trick unknown to him. It was pointless to tell him I had been invited for a drink because I had seemed not to be interested. If you showed lady luck the back of your hand, sometimes she came crawling.

Montgomery Clift, who was very sensitive to any vibes from or around Marilyn Monroe, came over to ask me why I hadn't taken him up on his invitation. How could I explain? If I wrote about him, I'd have to be true to my experience of him, and I didn't want to harm his career. If news of his drinking became well known, he might find it hard to get work because insurance companies would consider him too much of a risk. We agreed to get together before work was finished in Reno in a few days and everyone beat it back to Hollywood to complete the film there. His look seemed to ask if I really meant it. Another big star with this inner uncertainty. He and Marilyn Monroe seemed like brother and sister then.

A long bullfighting article by Hemingway had just appeared in *Life* magazine and several people were critical of it in a rather smart-ass way. Someone asked John Huston, a great Hemingway fan, what he thought of it. Huston said slowly, in his deepest voice, "I liked it." He said no more—no argument, nothing. That stopped the discussion. The ass-kissers didn't want to risk Huston's wrath. He was a serious Hemingway student. Hemingway's tough-guy life and stoic philosophy no doubt appealed to him very much. I remembered once asking Huston if living abroad in Ireland was dangerous to him as an artist, and he recalled that Hemingway hadn't lived in the U.S. since the first time he went to France. Miller had commented that Huston was so American, "he always would be, even if he lived on the moon."

I felt that I made no contact with Huston beyond his image. It was as though he had given himself a role to play written by himself, a role he felt safe with and one which was successful in Hollywood, and he didn't allow you to see him

66

outside it. Hemingway did much the same in his later years. It is a safe way to deal with strangers when you are famous.

But Marilyn Monroe gave the opposite impression. She was struggling to break out of the role Hollywood had written for her. Betty Grable hadn't managed it, but Marilyn was determined to succeed. That was what *The Misfits* was about to her: her big chance to convince the world that she was a real actress.

Gable seemed to be showing the strain more than she was. I noted in my diary: "Gable looked grey today, even when he had washed off the dust from the dry lake where they were filming. Usually talkative with his entourage, who gather around him like courtiers, he sat silent between shots on the steps of his camper. Somebody mentioned his wife's coming baby, generally a topic to brighten him at any time, but not even that stirred him today. Was the King sulking—which would be unlike Gable—or is he tired? If so, who could blame him? It is physically a very strenuous part for him. He revived a little when he told me a joke about his peak years in Hollywood as the Great Lover. A fussy woman who almost tried to rape him had upset him so much that he had taken out his false teeth and let her see his handsome face cave in without them. 'That cured her,' he said, chuckling. He is certainly a very unassuming, no-nonsense, professional star. Monroe could do with some of his detachment and self-confidence."

The strain on Monroe showed perhaps more in her marriage. My diary noted: "The Millers seem curiously detached from each other on the set. They rarely speak. M.M. has her entourage always with her (how different it is from Gable's), and A.M. talks with Huston, with the professional cowboys, with Gable, or broods alone on the fringe of everything—but is never with her now. It is a nervous period, this enactment

67

of high emotion in the Nevada desert, and probably husband and wife are better apart on the job, but there is the usual Hollywood gossip. How one grows to hate this gossip—it is like a disease that tries to destroy even the idea of innocence. . . ."

Miller invited me to dinner to watch the second Nixon-Kennedy TV debate with him. The first debate had been thoroughly analyzed by the political pros. TV political campaigning was still in its fledgling days and nobody seemed sure which was more important, the vision or the sound. It was agreed, however, that what was needed was "sincerity," which meant that the candidate must seem to believe what he was saying even if he didn't. Thus there was much more chance of "not achieving sincerity" if speakers engaged in tricky solo performances than if they played safe and settled down for a simple question-and-answer session with other people. Nixon and Kennedy had both decided to play safe.

Miller and I had a pleasant dinner, during which we both avoided the subject of *The Misfits*. The struggle between him and Huston to reach a common vision was impossible from the beginning, or so it seemed now. How lucky Chaplin and Ingmar Bergman were to be both director and writer of their films! I told Miller about my experience with the San Francisco hostess and, as he had been accused of being a Red himself, it seemed to make him more sympathetic toward Kennedy—or was that only because he disliked Nixon?

Nixon in the second TV debate made me remember Huston's "Who do they think we are?" Nixon relied far more on the vision than the sound. He stared with a sincere look while speaking wooden words like responsibility, security, welfare—which no longer meant much except as a reassurance to the unthinking that everything was all right. He seemed to have decided that his image was what was important, that the words should merely provide the right background. Kennedy often went to the opposite extreme. His image was frequently lost in a stream of precise information, including dates and names and other references. The result was that Nixon seemed to be fighting a comforting campaign that sounded positive—"The prestige of the United States has never been higher," and so on—but was essentially negative because it did not argue a case. Too often it played on prejudices (we must be tough with the Reds; any giving up of anywhere is selling out; to criticize the U.S. government is unpatriotic). Whereas Kennedy might be putting forward a more positive argument, he was often made to seem negative because he carped on what was wrong with the U.S. while Nixon repeated Eisenhower's everything's-all-right-Jack theme.

Miller shook his head sadly and asked if I knew the Lincoln-Douglas debates with which these debates had been compared. "Lincoln and Douglas would take a particular case," he said, "and in their argument apply it to their general philosophy. There's no attempt here to do anything of that kind. And there was no mention in either speech of the big problems like China. We can't go on not facing it. It's there, it's a fact, but we haven't yet faced it." He groaned over some of the Nixonisms, the meaningless language, the playing on prejudice, and then talked about the difference between written and oral words. "I used to think Adlai Stevenson often hadn't the oral touch. He was reading written prose, though a lot of my friends don't agree with me. Roosevelt had the oral touch. He appreciated the necessity for greater directness and the difference in speed. Truman did, too. He may not have been very eloquent sometimes, but it got through."

"I think I'll vote for a misfit," I said.

69

The door slammed and Marilyn Monroe came in. Well, that meant they were still together. Rumor, lie down. But there were no smiles this time for him or me. Miller looked up cautiously, as if trying to read her mood.

"Thank goodness you've brought someone home," she said in a cold voice. "You never bring any company. It's so dull," and she disappeared into the bedroom.

Miller looked as if he'd been struck. I felt sorry for him, and I didn't like that. I wasn't sure I liked her after all. She could certainly be a bitch. A lady with a bad temper.

Miller didn't refer to the incident and she didn't reappear. I left soon afterward. Miller was going to do yet another rewrite of the ending. He and Huston were disagreeing over how it should go. The collaboration must have begun to seem as burdensome as his marriage to Monroe. Huston apparently wanted the ending to be more explicit. If one had to choose a word for Hollywood's style, it would be *explicit.* Yet shouldn't an implicit meaning be the aim? It was very difficult to achieve that in the teamwork of a film. Miller wouldn't be in the best mood to achieve it after that brush with his wife. I imagined how she was feeling—lying in bed perhaps, irritable and dissatisfied.

She asked me the next day what I thought of Kennedy. There was no sign of the bitch of the night before. She was smiling and mischievous.

I replied carefully that I preferred Kennedy to Nixon.

She giggled. "It would be so nice to have a president who looks so young and good-looking." She seemed excited.

"You mean he has a Hollywood image," I teased her.

She was immediately defensive. "You must admit it's better than having old uglies who have no brains *or* beauty."

I remember this conversation and her subsequent involvement with the Kennedys when people write of her now as part of the nostalgia for the fifties, when she made most of her films. To me, she is much more representative of the restless, changing sixties—as Kennedy was.

I chatted with Paula Strasberg about the Method and the character of Roslyn. "Marilyn has had to find similar experiences in her own past to re-create the right emotion," she said, sitting in the white, dusty, dry lake in black clothes more suitable for the opera. She had various nicknames, including "The Witch." While we were talking, Marilyn was several yards away, lying on a table, being massaged by Ralph Roberts. Then she suddenly had her table moved much closer to us, as if she wanted to be the center of attention even then, for who could concentrate on an intellectual talk about the Method when Marilyn Monroe, almost nude, was being rubbed down close by? She wasn't classically beautiful by any means, but she had a strong, attractive body and chameleon moods that could make her body convey anything she wished.

Her entourage had been enthusiastically reading Lawrence Durrell's *Alexandria Quartet* and had pressed it on her as a modern masterpiece. She had obviously found it rather hard going. She asked me how I liked it. I said I found Durrell a little too wordy for my taste. I admired the first volume, *Justine,* but the others were too much like part of a word game one had already played. She grinned with relief, as if she had found an unexpected ally. At that moment, she looked so unlike the bitch who had cut down her husband in front of me, a comparative stranger now, and I was wary of her. She obviously had a large repertoire of moods, aspects, and roles. Miller had only conveyed part of her in the character of Roslyn—the nicer part? Was that what was really causing all the trouble in the script and for her in her performance?

We were near the end in Reno now, and she reminded me to call on Mrs. Chekhov when we went to Hollywood. I asked her who else I might talk to for a knowledge of the movie industry and of what she had had to overcome. She suggested one of the big old-time producers. I mentioned Sam Goldwyn. "Yeah, great," she replied, "if he'll see you. It's like trying to make an appointment with God." Who else? One of her other directors, Billy Wilder, I suggested. She grimaced. "If you like." And who else? One of the writers. She mentioned Clifford Odets. "They say he was sort of the Arthur of the thirties. He ran into the same kind of Red-baiting from that terrible committee in Washington that Arthur did. That was a time, I can tell you. Some of those bastards in Hollywood wanted me to drop Arthur, said it would ruin my career. They're born cowards and want you to be like them. One reason I want to see Kennedy win is that Nixon's associated with that whole scene."

Before I left Reno, I had a brief talk and drink with Montgomery Clift, but missed any long exploratory session. He talked a little of the dangers to the young of being good-looking. It made you into a Narcissus. The accident that had wrecked his face had not been all bad. "I had to try to master myself, find the real me outside my looks which people were hung up on and so was I." He said an aging homosexual in Hollywood was trying to "save" him from his drinking, but he didn't want any kind of involvements with people. He wanted to save himself. "I have the same problem as Marilyn. We attract people the way honey does bees, but they're generally the wrong kind of people. People who want something from us, if only our energy. We need a period of being alone to become ourselves. To be an actor, you can't afford defenses, a thick skin. You've got to be open, and people can hurt you easily."

I said I thought the character he played in *The Misfits* should go off with Marilyn in the end. He agreed. "Arthur was doing some wish-fulfillment. He identified with the character played by Gable. Arthur wanted him to keep Marilyn because he wants to himself. But their marriage is over, and he might as well face it. My character represented something new, the future—Marilyn's future. Maybe Marilyn and I would have got together one day if we weren't so much alike. As it is, it's too much like brother and sister getting together. That's what's wrong with Gable going off with her in the end. When Marilyn first went to Hollywood, Gable was a father figure to her. It's like a girl going with her father. No, Arthur's got it wrong. Maybe that's what's wrong with his relationship with her.

75

Maybe he was too paternal. I know she respected him too much, looked up to him. All idols fall eventually. Poor Marilyn, she can't keep anyone for long. . . ."

He ordered another drink, his face frowning as if he was suffering for her.

10

Mrs. Chekhov lived modestly in Los Angeles. Her husband could not have left much money, and I wondered if Marilyn helped out. She was to remember Mrs. Chekhov in her will.

An energetic, charming old woman with a sharp sense of humor, Mrs. Chekhov spoke warmly of Marilyn and of her kindness. She recalled how Marilyn had brought her new husband for a visit and Arthur Miller had given her a copy of his collected plays. She showed me the inscription—to one who had been so kind to his Marilyn. She talked of the marriage with real affection. "They are such a beautiful couple, so much in love." She obviously didn't know the marriage was in trouble. I steered the conversation away to safer topics.

She played some recordings of her husband's lectures. He came from the Stanislavsky tradition, like the Method people in New York, but he seemed less doctrinaire than they were, as if his approach were essentially that of the actor, the doer, rather than the teacher and preacher. Mrs. Chekhov said regretfully: "Now nobody remembers." I disagreed, mentioning *Spellbound.* "You say his name," Mrs. Chekhov replied, "and now no one here knows who he is except a few loyal admirers like Marilyn who keep his memory alive." She thanked me for remembering and said she would tell Marilyn about our meeting. "She is well?" she asked with concern. "I read in the newspapers that she was in a hospital." I said I had seen her two days before and she appeared very well then. "Thank God," she said.

The brief visit made a strong impression on me and I corresponded with Mrs. Chekhov after I left Los Angeles. Inevitably, I wondered about Marilyn's motives. She had obviously understood Mrs. Chekhov's need to hear praise of her husband. Did she also want to seem kind and considerate to a reporter, or was that being too cynical? I also had a strange feeling that she had been trying to show me something. She was a great admirer of Michael Chekhov, and yet here he was almost forgotten. Was she illustrating the fate of talent in Hollywood unless you fight and beat the system? That was my guess; that was what she herself was trying to do. She was a complicated woman, all right. How foolish those people were who underrated her as a dumb blonde! What I didn't yet know and couldn't guess was how much was natural—or as natural as a human being can be—and how much was a calculated performance. I was to learn.

Sam Goldwyn would see me, provided I promised to show him a transcript of the interview before I published anything. I hadn't been asked to do that since I interviewed a prime minister during an international crisis. At Goldwyn's level in the movie business, it was high politics, and Goldwyn was very sensitive about putting his foot in his mouth, mainly because journalists had mocked him for such "Goldwynisms" as the famous "include me out."

In the reception room, when I said I had an appointment with Sam Goldwyn, the heads shot up, the row of waiting heads you always found in Hollywood reception rooms. A woman with large Bette Davis eyes reacted as if the appointment were with God; she nudged her neighbor to make sure he had heard. Pathetic it might be as a human scene, but at least it was a tribute to Goldwyn's staying power as one of Hollywood's founding fathers.

Then in his fiftieth year "in the business," he must have felt lonely, for nearly all of his fellow Hollywood founding fathers had gone. DeMille had gone where the Ten Commandments came from. So had Louis B. Mayer. Chaplin was in Europe and would never come back to work. Mary Pickford had retired. But Goldwyn survived. It was fitting that he remained so loyal to the dream city he helped to found, for he was so representative of it.

He began as a businessman, an immigrant from Poland, not basically sympathetic to artists or even knowing much about the art of the cinema or the art of anything else except the art of survival in competitive America. The early films were commodities, consumer goods. He had one of the keenest pair of eyes in America for anticipating changes in taste and new markets and was usually at least half a step ahead of the customers, gambling on his salesmanship and the quality of his product to persuade them to keep up with him. Most of the Hollywood producers were such timid, unoriginal businessmen that they lagged a step or two behind public taste. So Goldwyn's success helped some of them become more adventurous and thus produce slightly better films. This was probably his major contribution to the development of Hollywood.

More and more he gained the confidence to look at himself as the test of what the public wanted. A sentimental man, as well as a shrewd one, he wanted love, loyalty, honor and family pride depicted in his films—the sort of themes that a whole family, from grandfather on down to a teenage grandson, might respond to (and pay for). Like a clever manufacturer, he realized that you needed the best craftsmen to produce the goods from your master plan. So he employed some of the most capable directors, actors, technicians, and screenwriters Hollywood had to offer or he could tempt from elsewhere, usually Broadway or Europe. It wasn't art; it couldn't be because of that master plan. But often it was superior family entertainment of a topical kind, the prize-winning *The Best Years of Our Lives* being one of the best examples.

He looked a little like a shrewder, tougher Eisenhower, an Eisenhower who had had to fight it out in big business instead of the safer, bureaucratic army. He was not a man who easily tolerated interruptions or arguments, and he sometimes impatiently answered a question when I was only midway through asking it. His toughness showed only once—when I had the temerity to disagree with his view that *South Pacific* was a great picture. He snapped back about how much it had grossed at the box office.

"A great picture," he said, "doesn't have to be a great spectacle. The spectacle comes from here," and he touched the front of his jacket. "From the heart."

I tried to get him to talk about the Hollywood treatment of artists. He took a paternal view.

"When I first started the Goldwyn company, I brought thirty-five of the best writers in the world out here. What I really attempted to do was to make the writers the stars. But no dice. They came out here, but instead of working for the Goldwyn company, they wrote pieces for the magazines or they wrote a book while they were collecting salaries from me. . . ."

Thinking of Marilyn Monroe and her problems, I asked him if the star system had changed. He didn't give me time to complete the question. I had wanted to relate my question to the typing of the stars, but Goldwyn cut me short: "I think in my entire career I have engaged no more than three or four who actually were stars. You take the case of Danny Kaye. He never acted in his life. He was an entertainer in a cafe; but as far as acting is concerned, that's a different medium completely. But I had patience and he developed, to my mind, to be one of the great comedians we have on the screen. I took Eddie Cantor. Paramount had sent him back to New York, but I believed in his ability, and he was a great success with me. You take Sir Laurence Olivier. I think he is one of the great actors we have. But a Shakespearean experience will not make you ready for motion pictures. To prove that, when he was out here for RKO or some other company, they sent him back to Europe. They did not exercise his option. He came here to do *Wuthering Heights*. To be very frank with you, at first he gave a Shakespearean performance and we had to do it over, and then he gave a very fine performance—as fine as I have had in a motion picture. He had to treat the medium a little differently from the stage. I have this theory, and it is a very strong one, that the star comes out of the story. I have seen some of the best stars we have fall on their behinds if they had a bad story. A star will not make a bad story good, but a good story will make a star great. If you have not got the scenes, you just fall on your behind. I have always preached that you start with the story and you finish with it. . . ."

When I told Marilyn Monroe the gist of this, she sighed and said: "What did I tell you? That's just what we're up against. By 'story,' they mean family entertainment." She was amused by the condescending remarks about Sir Laurence Olivier. She had met the great actor only at the height of his fame and had had an uneasy working relationship with him in *The Prince and the Showgirl*. It amused her to think that the great man she had met—and whom she considered patronising

—had gone through the Hollywood machine just as she had. "Sir Olivier," as she called Sir Laurence, "tried to be friendly, but he came on like someone slumming. He upset me a lot by telling me to"—and here she imitated his voice—" 'Look sexy, Marilyn.' It sounded condescending to me, like Goldwyn talking of him. I started being bad with him, being late, and he hated it. But if you don't respect your artists, they can't work well. Respect is what you have to fight for."

When I left a transcript of the long interview for Goldwyn, it was returned with the message that the meeting had been reported "as accurately as humanly possible," which gave me the impression that Goldwyn's standard was a celestial one.

·

Billy Wilder had directed her in *Some Like It Hot*, a slick, amusing satire in which she had begun to break away from type-casting. She had been late one day. According to legend, at least, she was reading Paine's *The Rights of Man* in her trailer. When an assistant director came for her, she told him to fuck off. More evidence of her bad temper beneath the blonde sweetness. It made her seem more human. She couldn't be that sweet and survive; perhaps the bad temper had saved her. But there had been ill will at the end of *Some Like It Hot*. Billy Wilder felt the strain of working with her, and a fellow star, Tony Curtis, had nothing complimentary to say.

When I met Billy Wilder, a small, balding, bouncy non-stop talker, he shrugged off a question about her. She could be a pain in the ass, but she was a real star. He was full of a plan to make a movie about the Marx Brothers at the United Nations. He was known as a good judge of how far the public was willing to let a satirist go—"My nightmare is playing to half-empty houses," he said—and he judged that the public was ready for a satire on the UN. He had estimated that he and his fellow scriptwriter, I.A.L. Diamond, needed 3,000 jokes. "The Marx Brothers will, of course, be the same as ever. They're older. They won't get the girl. But otherwise they won't change." The awful subplot which generally padded out the story between the Marx Brothers' inspired mad moments would be replaced by a serious, sophisticated subplot.

Wilder made a few wry comments about the Nixon-Kennedy campaign, adding that films about American politics played to half-empty houses. "They generally bore American audiences and are incomprehensible to non-American audiences." Why, then, was the UN different? "It's fun and it involves the world as a whole. It will be understood universally—therefore it's worth a film. Making a film is like gambling, with the chips getting more expensive every day. That way you can't afford too big a gamble. You need a universal subject. So we've got the UN and we've got the Marx Brothers. Put them together and—*boom!*"

The ideas were only just coming to the boil, so he ad-libbed a little. "Imagine, we might have the Marx Brothers mixing up all the flags with, say, Nasser coming in under the Star of David. Mad fun like that. People are so sick of the solemn approach that they're ready for this. We'll keep the same Marx Brothers technique of playing against a very serious background. We'll try to keep it all—the dignity of the locale, the procedure, the enormity of the problem—with Groucho, Harpo, and Chico in the middle of it."

But it was one of those Hollywood dreams that was never to be realized. Nothing came of the idea before death broke up the Marx Brothers. "He's a brilliant moviemaker," Marilyn told me when I described the meeting, "but he worries too much about the box office. A movie of his about the UN would have no real teeth. He'd be scared of politics and unpopularity. It's not the right subject for him."

I called on Clifford Odets soon after breakfast. He was a writer of the Depression and therefore was naturally angry and rebellious. But what was the Angry Young Man like twenty-five years later? Success had struck him. He had settled in Hollywood. He had lost some of his old friends when he cooperated with the House Committee on Un-American Activities in its Hollywood witch-hunt.

He received me warmly, openly, with an earnestness that was almost childlike. Just as I had been surprised by the girlish sensitiveness that had survived in Marilyn Monroe, so something about Odets, a successful screenwriter, reminded me astonishingly of a fledgling writer in a cold-water walk-up in the Village. Neither of them had been streamlined or made over, yet they had survived successfully. The Angry Young Man, though old now, was still angry, and about the same things. Sometimes his anger seemed archaic, as if he were still hitting at targets that no longer existed or had at least changed their position, almost as if he were trying to work himself up to the condition in which he did his best work. Many of the other writers of the Thirties were the same: writers trying to recapture their creative anger of yesterday in the cooling atmosphere of the Cold War. The moment of truth for many of them came with the trial of communism. Confessing to having been Communists, as if they were guilty of a crime, was like repudiating their past; communism had meant something different in the Depression. Odets admitted that he had been a Communist for a short time and had quit when he was told to write according to the party line. This seemed to be an admirable

86

artistic stand, but his critics attacked him on other grounds. They argued that he should have refused to cooperate as a gesture against McCarthyism, that his cooperation had helped the witch-hunt, and that the Angry Young Man had therefore betrayed his ideals. Was there some guilt now in his ready anger? Hollywood already had its share of martyrs, for good and sometimes bad reasons—film workers who were hounded out of the industry long after they had paid the penalty for refusing to give evidence against other people. But Odets, like most artists, was no more a martyr than he was a politician; his response was emotional rather than practical; he was with the Communists when they appeared to be in favor of a "better world" (he told Harold Clurman that he "wanted to belong to the largest possible group of humble, struggling men prepared to make a great common effort to build a better world"); he was against them when he realized that he had been used.

From being the author of an early play that showed "no trace of talent" (Clurman again), Odets became in the Thirties a Broadway success, the most promising of the younger dramatists. He was therefore worth using for various causes, Communist and Hollywoodish. One critic suggested: "Odets has lost his reason from too much brooding over the Marxist eschatology." He went to Hollywood and raised money for the Group Theater in New York, went back to Broadway, returned to Hollywood, had a stormy marriage to Luise Rainer. Clurman finally concluded that Odets had become "somehow unsure of everything; more bewildered in a way than he had ever been as the obscure young actor of our crazy company. Odets was now his own greatest problem." World War II ended the Thirties. The Communist dream in America blew up. The Group Theater collapsed. By then Odets was not alone among the Americans of the Thirties in being "unsure of everything."

Some of the writers went to Hollywood where they had to conform to studio standards. Some nearly drowned in bitterness. Perhaps Odets did both. At least the Angry Young Man of the Thirties was now so far from any party membership that he dismissed "the general gaseous talk of politicians all over the world."

As a dramatist he was a poetic realist, but often he kept too rigidly to the line of a plot for a deep development of character. *Golden Boy* provided a good example in its final scenes: all problems were solved by killing off the hero. Melodrama forced the pace too much. With this strict adherence to plot line came the temptation to substitute a pinch of propaganda for plot; thus talent was sometimes bent for a quick return. Did Hollywood take over as the temptress after politics?

Odets himself denied it. For him, his swimming pool was not a symbol of capitulation but an investment. The Hollywood it stood for would finance his return to New York to write several plays he had already planned in detail.

"Most of them deal with contemporary themes which have to do with the great question of what is democracy, how shall we live, how shall we use life, particularly today in our atomized world. I'm doing them in the form of thrillers and I can almost feel the quality of them. What I am today is based on what I was in the thirties and forties, but I feel over the years I have become a more subtle, mature human being. What I want to express now can no longer be done in the realistic three-act plays in the Ibsen form. I have to search for new forms."

It was to be another unrealized Hollywood dream, like Billy Wilder's Marx-Brothers-at-the-UN. Odets was to die a Hollywood man. He postponed going back for too long. But the day I talked to him, the dream was clearly important. It was a sustaining dream, lifting him out of the unsatisfactory past and present. He gave the impression not of querulousness —like so many middle-aged authors—but of a too-sensitive man still without armor.

He told me beside his swimming pool: "The English Lloyd George used to say politicians were apt to start hares. I think all over the world politicians are starting hares for us to run after. I don't give a goddam if we get to the moon or not. We have a basic problem that needs a president like Lincoln to face it. Several presidents refused to face the issue of the Civil War. They found political and ideological reasons not to look at it. Then along came a man like Lincoln who said, 'This is what's got to be done and I'm the man who has to take it all over. God help me. Here I go.' So today we have a similar problem in America—of similar proportions anyway—and let's hope we have a similar man."

He paused and glanced across the swimming pool and then rushed on: "What's the problem? In America—I won't talk about the rest of the world—the problem is 'are peace and plenty possible together with the democratic growth to use them?' Look what we've had. Truman had admirable qualities, but he was a small man alongside Roosevelt. He built up, along with Russia, something called the Cold War which made prosperity possible. If it didn't continue, in six to ten months we would have ten to twelve million unemployed people. So we have learned to take the old-fashioned plenty that war always brought, in so-called Cold War conditions, which keep industry grinding. But still the basic problem has not been faced. The liberals are fooled; everybody is fooled. The extraordinary cynicism of politicians all over the world has twisted the heads of people and made them jittery. I'm not smart enough to know the answer, but there are politicians who have begun to look in other contexts.

" 'Peace and Plenty and the Grace to use them'—that was what William Penn said. The next step would be to find out how we fulfill in each individual citizen the profound promises of Jeffersonian democracy. And when this is achieved, many international problems will automatically be solved.

"I don't know how to write about that," added the Angry Old Man, suddenly becoming the dramatist again. "I have only got to give a sensitive reflection of what is hurting, agonizing me. That's all I have to offer as a writer."

On the way out he asked me about *The Misfits*. He described Miller as "a very serious man" and Monroe as "a uniquely American woman—half femme fatale and half child." He asked about her performance in *The Misfits*, seeing it as her first real dramatic role. "I hope my old Group Theater buddies don't make her too self-conscious," he said referring to Lee Strasberg, who was in the old Group Theater and now headed the Actors Studio, the Method center where Marilyn took lessons.

We stood at his front door in the hot California sunshine and Odets told me: "Why don't you come round and use my pool if you haven't got one?"

I saw Marilyn next day at the studio, preparing to film the last scene. The last rewrite still had Gable getting the girl; maybe Montgomery Clift was right, and wishful thinking had won. She asked me about my visit with Odets. She was defensive about the Strasbergs' influence on her when I quoted his remark, but it also seemed to amuse her. "He sounds like a nice man," she said. "A bit like Arthur, but more emotional."

"Want to use his pool?" I said.

"No, one writer at home is enough to deal with. Too much, in fact." She gave me a searching look, as if to see whether I understood what she was hinting at. I thought I did. She hurried on: "Mrs. Chekhov said she enjoyed your visit." The two women were obviously in close touch. "You know something?" she added. "You've been seeing the famous. Now you ought to see the unknowns, those who are trying to make it. That's the real Hollywood. Try Schwab's."

I went there the next day. It was the most depressing sight in Marilyn's Hollywood, the daily gathering of young hopefuls at Schwab's drugstore. Perched like starlings over their Coca-Colas and hamburgers, they chattered their mock tales of woe about producers ("Wouldn't even see me"), about agents ("He can't be trying"), about their awful, incredibly bad luck so far. They consoled themselves and each other with endless repetition of the legends of how stars were made overnight. Surely it might happen to them. "Jimmy Darren, man, was spotted while he was waiting for an elevator and now he's on his way to being a Big Star. Eddie's brother came out on vacation and a talent scout saw him in Schwab's and now he's got a contract with—I forget which studio, but one of the big ones. And *he* —dammit—hadn't even been *trying* to get in the movies."

So the would-be's went on interminably, and under their dream-spinning were the nagging postcards from home asking for news of them ("You haven't written home, Norma, for six long weeks. Is anything wrong. . . ?"). Nothing wrong that they dared recognize, and no news good enough to send back to the hundred big and little American towns which they had left so optimistically not long ago.

This youthful concentration, formidable enough, was modest compared to the flocks that came during Hollywood's boom years, when every high school actress saw herself as one of a hundred stars. That was when Marilyn was starting out. There were no longer a hundred stars left; the facts of film life must have made some impression on even the dreamers. This studio was making no films "at present," that one was now a factory for TV serials; the empty sound stages seemed to mock all hopes. If you dreamed of being a star now, you should see yourself as another Ty Hardin in *Bronco* on TV or as a TV femme fatale in *77 Sunset Strip*. Television, not movies, offered what hope there was. Yet the talk in Schwab's was still of stars like Monroe and Brando; you might do TV work for rent money, but every Method man, every pretty blonde, every new arrival from some little town, saw his future in Monroe, in Brando, in the few stars still left. Raise a doubt and back they went to Jimmy Darren, man, to Eddie's brother, to all the rest. An agent's quick glimpse could still change your luck and your life; so the careful wardrobes, the regular examinations in the snack-bar mirrors, the indispensable comb in back-trouser pockets, the peacock touch.

Every actor has a Narcissus instinct which he holds tightly in check if he has any sense. But here there seemed to be excesses, dangerous ones, for the temptation to the most beaten of the failures was to live off their looks. Hollywood, the dream capital, had its nightmare depths waiting to suck them down. I felt like saying to these charming, self-centered children whose vanity, if not talent, had brought them here: "Go home before it's too late." But perhaps once they had arrived, it was already too late to leave. Around them, if they looked, were enough examples from the Thirties and Forties and Fifties—the would-be's of another generation, spoiled now through disillusion, who waited behind the counters, drove the cabs, policed the streets, who had failed to "get into pictures" but realized it too late. To go back home meant to admit failure; to stay at least meant having a Hollywood address. You could half live your dream. Reality was far away, at least as far as downtown.

I told Monroe about my experience. "Now you've graduated," she said with a giggle. "You've seen where we come from and what we have to fight and what happens to some of us. When I starred in my first movie, I went back to Schwab's. I had the idea it would help their confidence to see someone who had gotten a break. But no one recognized me and I was too shy to tell anyone. I was a misfit there!"

11

I saw half the film in a Hollywood projection room. It was the first time Arthur Miller had seen the scenes strung together. At the end there was the usual embarrassed pause, then Miller murmured: "You know, it's at least an unusual movie, in one way. I've just seen that I've left out the conventional plot. All the characters do is react on each other."

A voice boomed from the back: "That's its strength, Arthur."

Another fruity Hollywood baritone added: "You've got a great movie here, Arthur."

Miller looked pained, as if he knew the voice could be relied on to say that, whatever the film. Huston and Monroe and Gable weren't there. They were in a studio nearby, shooting the last scene. Miller had done the final version, whether he liked it or not. Gable still got Monroe.

When we came out into the daylight, Miller asked me what I thought of Monroe's performance. I praised it and he seemed pleased. He was obviously still very fond of her. It was the final scenes, however, that would test her as an actress, and as I had watched them being filmed, I wondered if she was trying too hard, was too self-conscious. But maybe it would look different on the screen. I didn't say anything to Miller.

I watched the last scene being completed. Monroe and Gable sat in a car. Although neither of them knew it, this was the last scene for both of them—the last scene of their last film. Gable died soon afterward, and Monroe never completed another. But that day they looked as happy as everyone else, happy that the long, arduous work on *The Misfits* was almost over at last. Why do we want to know the future?

Everyone was tired and planning some kind of vacation; Gable seemed more tired than anyone else. He had been famous for his aggressive look of vitality, but now he seemed almost delicate. It was a sentimental last scene and it still didn't seem right, but the film was already well behind schedule, and Miller and Huston were probably too weary of it to solve any further problems now. Stalemate for the collaboration.

Huston now was brisk and businesslike. I wondered what he had planned once his work was done; his manner suggested it was something good. Two photographers were driving to the Grand Canyon and invited me to go along, but I already had my eyes on New Orleans. Integration was due to begin in the schools there and an explosion was expected in the segregated city: a drama in reality instead of in a movie. I'd get Hollywood —and Monroe—out of my head.

When I stood close to her, I could see blemishes beneath the clever makeup. She looked as if she'd missed a lot of sleep. She asked me if I'd like to have a last drink, but I explained I was rushing away to New Orleans. "Maybe I'll see you in New York, then," she said with a dazzling smile.

"I hope so," I said weakly. It seemed unlikely. Our paths weren't likely to cross even if we were in New York at the same time. I still felt a great curiosity about her. She had made an effort to be friendly, and I wondered why. I still distrusted the motives of celebrities who wooed any reporter. But she hadn't avoided showing me her bad side and that was certainly unusual. It was like half understanding a sphinx, half solving a complex problem. But that was a reporter's life. You arrived for a short time, grabbed a few fast impressions, and were off again. Yesterday, Reno; today, Hollywood; tomorrow—New Orleans. Like a sailor, you couldn't afford to become too interested in anyone or any subject. My last view of Marilyn Monroe was of her back, walking away. She didn't have beautiful legs.

12

The Greyhound bus I traveled on was stopped in New Mexico and we all had to get out and answer police questions. They were pursuing someone, but of course they didn't explain. Cops love secrecy as much as criminals. For me, after my recent experiences, it was too much like a Hollywood scene come to life. When one young cop found out I was a reporter, he asked very seriously: "Do you think Senator Kennedy is correct in saying that this country is falling behind?" Maybe people were starting to listen, and Kennedy had a chance.

Segregation was still official in many parts of the South then. I encountered my first separate lunch counters and separate bathrooms. And when I was invited to an "integration party," it was as secret as a Resistance party in Paris during the German occupation.

The address was a house on a dark side street in the French Quarter. You had to knock a special way and satisfy a guard at the door that you were "a friend." Half the guests were black, half white; perhaps it was the sense of shared danger that made the party go with a bang until approaching dawn.

I was introduced to a young black woman named Christine. She was sceptical at first, and I was embarrassed. She asked me where I was from. I mentioned *The Misfits*—it seemed like a good, safe subject. She said Marilyn Monroe was about the only white American film star who interested her. "She's been hurt. She knows what the score is, but it hasn't broken her." I said she wasn't unique in that. Christine replied: "Most of the others pretend everything is peachy. They act like people acting, people who've made it."

"You don't think you're just reacting to all you've read about Marilyn Monroe—"

I'd intended to tease, but she said sharply, annoyed: "I don't read the gossip stuff. That's what comes out of her movies. She's someone who was abused. I could identify with her. I never could identify with any other white movie star. They were always white people doing white things."

"Not even with Bette Davis or—"

"Look"—she was suddenly irritated—"Us Negroes don't appear in movies as anything but symbols, Uncle Toms, because white audiences aren't supposed to be able to identify with Negroes. Well, what they can't do, we can't either."

As a result of this conversation and a subsequent friendship with the tough-talking Christine, I saw much of the civil rights movement in the South as an attempt to break out of being type-cast. Blacks had been more rigidly typed than Monroe and needed even more courage, talent, and ingenuity to overcome it. When I saw the angry white mob outside a school, yelling at the two little black girls in their best dresses, I imagined a fantasy in which these faces were in Hollywood, representing what Marilyn—and Betty Grable and the rest— had to contend with. Money was at the back of it all. What happened in New Orleans related to Hollywood, and vice versa. A society was consistent.

I spoke to the local federal judge, J. Skelly Wright, who had ruled in favor of integration. I had to show proof of my identity three times before I reached him in his office in the federal building. Our talk was interrupted several times by people who telephoned, wishing to tell that "nigger-loving" judge what they thought of him. The judge coolly told them that they must have the wrong number. This was his hometown, and in their eyes he was a traitor. In our talk he searched for what had given him "my mature and great sympathy for Negroes." Suddenly his memory seemed to throw it up, and he began to tell of one Christmas party in his office, how amid the gaiety he looked out of the window at a blind people's building opposite and saw that the blind people were having a party, too, but as they arrived, they were being separated into black and white. "They couldn't see to segregate themselves. . . ." It had been years before, but it still moved him so much that he had to turn his chair away from me and cover his face.

I was still in the South for election day, when Kennedy narrowly won over Nixon. Was that a victory for change, for nonconformity, for less type-casting? We wouldn't know for many months. The newspapers naturally were full of it and had little space for an item that in normal times would have been given big headlines. Marilyn Monroe announced that she and her third husband were separating, but she added that she hadn't hired an attorney and had no immediate plans for a divorce.

I had arranged to meet with Arthur Miller in New York, so I wrote, asking him if he wanted to cancel the meeting. No, he replied, telling me not to be too sensitive. By now it would be old news to him, news he had learned to live with. The rumors had been right, and he had done his anguishing during *The Misfits*. No wonder he never got the ending right; it was a wonder he could write at all. But I was more concerned about her than him. He was a self-reliant man, but she needed someone—a husband or a father figure, *someone* who seemed to care—a home, not a bachelor apartment. She would lean more on Paula Strasberg and on her entourage; it would leave her much more vulnerable. But then I remembered her bitch side. She could look after herself. I had my own troubles.

Christine and I met in secret at a seedy bar near the docks, where we had a brush with the police, and I had to disguise myself to get out of it. After that, we met in the huge, ornate New Orleans cemeteries, where the graves resembled marble temples and you could read the history of white New Orleans in their inscriptions. Then it was time to leave again.

13

Arthur Miller was living at the Chelsea Hotel on West 23rd Street. It was an old-fashioned, comfortable hotel that had a reputation for being nice to artists, especially writers. The entrance had plaques commemorating such famous residents as Thomas Wolfe, Dylan Thomas, and Brendan Behan.

Miller had an apartment there and seemed comfortably relaxed, little changed from when I had last seen him in Hollywood. Marilyn's name came up only once, and he seemed unaffected by it. He had turned the page and begun another chapter of his life without her, though I pitied his next wife if there was one: Marilyn would haunt him for a long time. But as the months rolled by, maybe he'd be relieved to be his own man again, away from her problems.

He gave me a copy of the book of *The Misfits*, dedicated to the late Clark Gable, who didn't know how to hate. Gable had died of a heart attack while I was in the South. I didn't remember him the way Miller did. I could imagine Gable hating vigorously, but it would be someone or something worth hating, like one of the more vicious producers or studio heads, the people who stifled the actors, the artists. But what I remembered most about Gable was his hearty, joyful, self-confident smile, which became something of a trademark in his films. I had rarely seen it during *The Misfits*. He had been as tired as he looked. I wondered how Marilyn had received the news of the death of her old father figure. Miller–Gable: it was all loss. A lot would ride on the success of *The Misfits*, the symbol of her escape from the old Hollywood.

Miller must also have been relieved that the other collaboration, the one with Huston, was over. He had been dependent on Huston's approval as the director, and now he was free. The theater must have seemed very enticing after his grueling Hollywood experience. If he married again, his new wife might be from Broadway, but surely not from Hollywood. Would he ever make another film? *The Misfits* had too many bad memories.

Miller and Tennessee Williams were often compared—they were the leading contemporary dramatists and had become well known at about the same time—but when I went to see Tennessee Williams in his New York apartment, he seemed to have more in common with Marilyn than with Miller. He was as open as she often seemed to be and he was a nervous talker, with a crazy streak that probably helped free his imagination. A small, round man—as different from the tall, lean Miller as he could be—he made Miller seem very reserved and self-controlled. He talked enthusiastically about Marilyn as "a golden girl" and as a comedienne. One remark he made could well have come from her. He complained that in the rehearsals for his current play on Broadway, *Sweet Bird of Youth*, he had been inundated with notes suggesting changes "from somebody other than the director" and they had demoralized him, sapped what was left of his self-confidence. But, I said, hadn't his great success made his self-confidence impregnable? He gave a high, hysterical laugh and said: "I have no self-confidence at all. I don't have any opinion about anything I have done for years after it is finished. I read that Eugene O'Neill always said anything he was working on was the finest thing he had ever written. I always feel it is the worst. I find it is a terrible disadvantage because you need confidence to create energy, the necessary vitality to push the thing through." I could imagine Marilyn saying that about her feelings on *The Misfits.* Williams also said that as a boy he had discovered writing as an escape from a world of reality in which he felt acutely uncomfortable. "Another thing I have always been haunted by—a fear, an obsession, that to love a thing intensely is to be in a vulnerable position where you may well lose what you most want." I was sure Marilyn would have seconded that.

Tennessee Williams introduced me to James Baldwin, not then famous but a struggling writer in the Village. Like Christine in New Orleans, he identified with Marilyn even though she was white. She'd been used, abused; he didn't seem at all interested in Miller. I felt like asking Baldwin what I had asked Christine—was he referring to the real Marilyn or to the image? But that was too easy. If I ever met Marilyn again, I'd ask her why so many blacks identified with her. I wondered what her answer would be. Probably not one I expected.

I had arranged to attend sessions at her alma mater, the Actors Studio, but it never occurred to me that I would meet her there. I supposed she was in hiding somewhere, nursing her wounds from the marriage breakup.

14

The *Manchester Guardian* opened most cultural doors in America because intellectuals respected the newspaper even if they had never read it. Lee Strasberg, director of the Actors Studio and chief teacher of the Method, made it clear to me that he was doing me a great favor, but at last he allowed me to attend the twice-weekly, open sessions. One or two actors and actresses presented a scene and then explained what they were trying to accomplish in it. Then anyone else in the informal class or audience could comment or criticize, and finally Strasberg summed up. It was casual on the surface. The attendance invariably included some well-known faces. When I went there for the first time, Paul Newman, who was on Broadway in *Sweet Bird of Youth*, attended the session, watching and listening closely but seldom speaking. Once more, the stars were students. In a sense, the only star there was Lee Strasberg.

A small man in dark clothes, he came in like a professor flanked by devoted students. He sat on the front row next to a young man with a tape recorder ready to switch on as soon as Strasberg began to speak. It would have been off-putting for a less self-confident man, but Strasberg gave the impression of enormous self-assurance, the kind one associates not with a human being but with a messenger of the gods. I suppose Strasberg really had a sense of mission, of bringing light to the chaotic darkness in which most actors prepared for their life's work. His comments were always thoughtful, sometimes ruthlessly analytical, his humor very much that of a pedagogue. If you admired him and accepted the Method, he seemed like a genius of a teacher; if you didn't, he seemed arrogant and sometimes absurdly dogmatic.

I watched Shelley Winters play a scene and then explain her aims and methods. She talked to her fellow actors almost too humbly and with an air of confession. By the end of her explanation, tears were rolling down her cheeks. She was as self-conscious as someone talking for the first time to a psychiatrist. I remembered Clifford Odets' remark when he wondered if Marilyn would be made too self-conscious. Watching stage actors in rehearsal and behind the scenes at performances, I have always been impressed by how tough they have to become —without losing their sensitiveness. However they feel, they have to be ready to go on every night at a certain time, often working out of miserable dressing rooms and in close proximity to other people. The Method's kind of detailed analysis opened one up, but did it help to cope with the practical details, to grow that tough side if one didn't have it already? I didn't doubt that Marilyn Monroe was a talented actress and could perform on stage, but I wondered if she could discipline herself to do so night after night in the comparatively rough-and-ready conditions of a theater.

Movie actresses have it easy. Schedules can be rearranged, retakes cover mistakes, you don't need to know all your lines at once, there are long rest periods and many assistants. Going from the movies to the stage is like going from first-class air travel to a stage-coach ride. All the comments I heard from Paula Strasberg, Lee Strasberg, and others about Marilyn Monroe's potential as a stage actress referred to her talent, never to whether, in her midthirties, she could cope with the practical details night after night. Let her be an hour or two late just once and she'd find that the show had gone on without her.

Perhaps they were all living a dream—yet another Holly-wood dream—or perhaps she could adapt herself and they were right. But watching Shelley Winters with tears running down her face made me worry that this kind of situation for Marilyn would only develop the qualities she already had too much of and not provide the ruthless self-control and tough endurance she needed. I remembered that fine stage actors like Marlon Brando were apparently softened up by the easier working methods of Hollywood and could never bring themselves to return to the hard grind of the theater.

I was sitting at the end of a row when the man next to me, whose face I didn't recognize, said something to someone about "Marilyn." When I glanced down the row, I saw her sitting three seats away from me, dressed in a disguise—a scarf around her hair, a blouse and slacks, and no makeup. I didn't show that I'd recognized her. Maybe she wouldn't want to remember me now or maybe she wanted to be as anonymous as possible. It was probably part of her pride (as it seemed to be Paul Newman's when I saw him there) to be no more prominent than the other students and give Strasberg the entire spotlight. I turned away and watched Strasberg talking with Olympian calm to a middle-aged woman who was sitting at his feet with a humble expression you could have seen from the balcony. It seemed like the brilliant performance of a dedicated student. Did actors ever stop acting?

Suddenly someone touched my hand. I looked up and Marilyn was leaning across the other people. "Hi," she said, smiling. We shook hands across them. My stock immediately went up with my neighbors and they gave me a close look in case they had failed to recognize some famous face. No, I was a nobody; Marilyn must be slumming.

We had no time to talk because the session had begun.

A reverential hush descended as Strasberg called everyone to attention with a quiet "Okay." He wasn't a distinguished-looking man physically; you wouldn't have glanced twice at him in the garment district or the Village. But he had an actor's physical discipline and a teacher's aura of authority. He was also an immensely articulate man. Even experienced actors might be scared of a tongue-lashing from him, though the most I ever heard him dish out was a sarcastic thrust or two which had such a strong effect that no more was needed. He behaved and was treated as though he were Moses come down from the mountain. This was the teacher as priest and psychiatrist. I could see his strong appeal for Marilyn Monroe. Not only did this experienced man of the theater take her stage ambitions seriously and see her as a great actress, unlike those Hollywood morons, but his method of teaching drew out her personal problems and turned him into a confessor, a support, a father she had never had. Her mother had gone into a mental hospital when she was a child and she still visited her, but she had never known her father. Was Strasberg a substitute or was he helping her through the loneliness left by the break with Miller?

I watched her watch Strasberg. Every time he spoke, she sat forward. Once her finger went into her mouth, like the most impressed of students before the great man. She listened intently, laughing readily at all his wry teacher jokes, sometimes nodding in serious agreement with him, occasionally, it seemed, even making a note of one of his pearls of wisdom. No teacher could have hoped for closer attention. I hoped Marilyn wasn't riding for another fall, that this wasn't another "idol," as Montgomery Clift had put it, who would eventually fall off the pedestal she had put him on and take part of her with him. Wasn't this devotion excessive for a woman in her midthirties? Or was Marilyn still so insecure that she was desperate to be taken seriously by people she admired in the arts? Or was she simply giving a performance, showing how modest a big star could be in the presence of a great teacher? Part of me was still sceptical of her. I had been delighted when she recognized me and spoke. Why? It wasn't attention from a celebrity; it was merely that I liked her. But I didn't want to fall for her charm, her professional seduction, as some other journalists had. So at the end of the session I didn't go over to speak to her but prepared to leave. She left a woman she was talking to and came over—rather tentatively, as if there was a chance of rejection. God, had she still got that kind of inferiority complex? I felt that I had been arrogant and rude and that by coming over, she was teaching me a lesson in politeness.

"Are you free for a drink?" I said, expecting her to make an excuse.

"I've got to get my hair done. It's a mess." Her hand went up to her scarf. "But how about later this afternoon?"

"Fine."

"Where? I could meet you in a bar. Anywhere will do."

"There's a bar around the corner on Eighth Avenue."

"Okay." She took the name.

She flashed me a smile and was gone. I had been so taken by her manner that I was hardly aware of how she looked. It now occurred to me that the bar I named might not be her style. It was a simple drinker's bar. But we could easily go somewhere else if she didn't like it. And then again, she just might not show up. I didn't see her as Miss Reliable.

15

When she was half an hour late, I decided she wasn't coming. Why the hell had she bothered to make the date? But I reminded myself that she had been several hours late on *The Misfits* and that had been more important. How long should I give her? I usually gave people a half hour, but this time I was unwilling to leave after thirty minutes, so I decided to give her an hour.

I had chosen a booth in the back where the lighting was dim, so no one would recognize her and we could talk. It was one of those simple bars with no table service, so I went up to the bar for another drink. If Marilyn was very late, I'd be drunk by the time she got there. But I was convinced by that time she'd either forgotten—the scatterbrained dumb blonde of legend (disappointment was making me nasty)—or she'd decided she couldn't make it on time and so would skip it and make apologies the next time we met at the Actors Studio.

For the first half hour I had kept my eyes on the swinging doors in the distance, but then the bar had become crowded and I'd given up and given all my attention to my drink and my thoughts about an article I was writing about Christopher Isherwood. I'd interviewed him when I was in Hollywood.

"A dollar for your thoughts," a voice said. A female voice. A familiar one.

"Not worth it," I said, looking up.

There she was, dressed the same way she had been at the Actors Studio, except that the head scarf was different and tied

123

much more loosely. A little of her hair showed. She was smiling gaily, like someone intent on having a good time. Just seeing her there certainly made my spirits rise.

I glanced around, a little embarrassed. Maybe a smart hotel bar was more her style, like the one we'd drunk in in Reno. "We can go to another bar—"

"No, no, I like it." She sat facing me, grinning. "I'm not often taken to a *real* bar."

"What'll you have to drink?"

"What are you drinking?"

"Gin and tonic."

"Okay, I'll try that."

I didn't know whether that meant she'd never had one before, or whether she'd see how this particular bar made one, or whether, to be friendly, she was having one because I was. I got it from the bar as quickly as I could, feeling strangely responsible for her there. I didn't want anyone to bother her.

"What were you thinking about?" she said. "You were very far away."

I explained about Christopher Isherwood. She knew the part of Santa Monica where the writer lived. She became most interested in something Isherwood had told me. It had been mystical and, to me, a little hard to grasp, but she seemed to follow immediately, as if it was close to one of her own ideas. I got out my notebook to read Isherwood's exact words to her: "I didn't decide to live here. It just happened, as with all the places I've lived. One grows older and changes, but one also changes with the places a little. If one didn't grow old and die, and if one could just be kept in a state of being at the physical age of about 35 or 40, I think one would probably go back and forth over a pattern of selves. But as we don't have the experience, it's impossible to tell."

She liked that—"a pattern of selves." She thought many people made the mistake of thinking of themselves as one consistent self during their entire lives. How much more tolerant they would be of other people if they understood their own fragmentary, changing natures! "I certainly change with places and people. I'm different in New York than I am in Hollywood. I'm different here in this bar than at the studio. But the same happens with people. I'm different with Lee than with my secretary, and I'm different again with you. I always see that in interviews. The questions demand certain answers and make you seem a certain kind of person. The questions often tell more about the interviewer than the answers do about me."

"You seduce interviewers." I grinned to show I wasn't attacking her. "You don't want them to get at the real you, but to fall in love with you and write love stories."

"You think so?"

"Oh, yes." Still grinning, unsure of her.

"Well, it didn't work with you. I had to come over to talk with you."

"Professional pride."

"Okay, I like it better. I don't respect people who like you because you're famous. If I was unknown, they wouldn't be interested."

"Maybe in a different way. Isherwood also said: 'What is very important is not to repudiate anything you have ever been, but to realize you will change and to accept it.'"

"Just repudiate other people and start again."

"People who don't like you say you discard people too easily."

That was a hard remark to make on such a short acquaintance, and she frowned at the thought that there were people who didn't like her. "I've never dropped anyone I believed in.

My trouble is, I trust people too much. I believe in them too much and I go on believing in them when the signs are already there. You get a lot of disappointments." She sat back, gloomy with memories. I mentioned hurriedly that Charles Laughton had a house next door to Isherwood's, knowing that she and Laughton had appeared together in the movie, *O. Henry's Full House*. Her mood changed immediately and her whole face brightened.

She leaned forward confidingly, full of fun. "He played a gentleman bum and I was a lady streetwalker." She giggled. "I was overawed at first, but he was very nice to me. He accepted me as an equal. I enjoyed working with him. He was like a character out of Charles Dickens." She looked at me with a strange expression, almost like a student seeking approval, and her voice became more like the little-girl tone she used in some of her movies—the defenseless blonde, the overawed young actress. She was playing a scene, teasing me. "At first I felt it was like acting with a king or somebody great—like a god!"

"That's the impression I get of Lee Strasberg," I said, testing her.

"Oh, Lee's not like that—not when you know him and he's interested in your work. But I guess he overawed me, too, at the beginning."

"He's not like a Dickens character?"

"No, Lee's made himself. He's not like anybody."

I recalled that when I'd interviewed Laughton a couple of years before, he'd told me: "People have seen every aspect of me by now and they know what to expect—old Laughton cooked up."

She smiled, showing teeth that were not as film-star white as I expected. "He didn't really believe that, but I can understand him feeling that way. I sometimes feel like that and I'm much younger than he is. I sometimes feel as if I'm too exposed. I've given myself away, the whole of me, every part, and there's nothing left that's private, just me alone. If you feel low, you might worry that there's nothing new to give. But that's not true—not ever. You discover things inside yourself you never knew were there. You always go on developing. A teacher like Lee helps you to uncover all the secret sides of yourself." She ended rather breathless, watching me eagerly for my response, as if it really mattered to her.

"It doesn't make you too self-conscious? You remember the story of the centipede who wondered how he did it—and fell over his own feet."

She laughed merrily. "Lee would hate that story. You've got to understand what you're doing. You've got to know yourself."

She was very defensive about Strasberg. It was better to stay off the subject, at least for now. I went back to Laughton because he seemed to interest her. I recalled that his wife Elsa Lanchester, a rather plain woman but a good character actress, had come in while we were talking, and Laughton, like a smoldering volcano, had said to me in a gruff, challenging voice: "Don't you think my wife's pretty?"

Marilyn liked that. She laughed so loudly that some people at the bar peered back at us. "He was being a loyal husband. They were married a long time, weren't they?"

"Twenty or thirty years, I think."

"I wish I could achieve a settled relationship like that," she said wistfully. "Someone always to come home to, someone always interested in what you're doing—and helping you over the tough spots, helping each other. I've come to love that line, 'until death do us part.' It always seems to go well for a time, and then something happens. Maybe it's me."

She meant it to sound joking, but she looked so sad about it, as though she'd touched a sore spot, that I hurried on with a Laughton postscript. It was four o'clock in the afternoon when I met him, but he was still in his bathrobe, his hair awry, sleep still in his eyes. When I described him that way in the article I wrote about him, he phoned me, very indignant. Readers would think actors were lazy, he said. He'd been up "for hours."

Marilyn chuckled, no longer sad. "He was only being defensive. I understand him. People have such strange ideas about actors. They seldom respect you. I recently met a suburban couple and the woman acted as if I was there to seduce her husband. She insisted on sitting between us. I wasn't respectable in her eyes."

"But don't you try to seduce every man you meet?" I was trying to keep her in a joking mood. "Don't you like to feel your power over them?" I said it humorously, but I meant it.

"Sometimes I hate the effect I have on people. I get tired of stupid attention, of working people up. It's not really a human thing." As if fearing that that sounded too self-pitying, she touched my notebook, still open at my notes of the Isherwood interview. "I hope our little drink isn't going in that notebook."

"Oh, no." I drew back, a little offended. Surely she could trust me more than that.

She touched my hand impulsively. "I was only joking. If I didn't trust you, I wouldn't be here. Don't be hurt so easily. I thought you reporters were supposed to be hard-boiled, like us Hollywood actresses. You're the first shy reporter I've ever met. You're like me—an old softie. I liked the way you went to see Mrs. Chekhov, but you didn't immediately run off and write about it. Put me in the notebook if you like, but don't write about it now. Do it when I retire!" She said it with a mocking smile—mocking herself?

"I'll retire before you—or be dead."

"Oh, no, you look too healthy." She smiled happily. She was in a smiling mood, as if trying to raise her own spirits, as well as mine. But everything she said seemed to turn strangely serious. She gave me the impression of a child whistling (or laughing) in the dark. The more she tried to cheer herself up, the more she seemed aware of the dark around her, threatening her. "What have you been doing since I saw you in Hollywood?"

I could have answered the question with some flip remark, but the only real compliment I ever paid her to her face was always to reply seriously to anything she said. I sensed that she thought too many people didn't take her seriously. She also seemed to pay me (and everyone else) the same compliment. When she was with you, she gave you her whole attention.

I tried to explain what had happened in New Orleans.

"Money," she said. "That's what it's all about. It's easy to understand the slave system when you've been through the star system." She asked me about Christine. "I once had an affair with a young Negro man," she said seriously. "He would never meet me in public—and I don't think I wanted to. I think we were both too scared. I used to sort of sidle into his room when nobody was looking. We liked each other. He understood me very well. But it couldn't last in those conditions. It was like trying to love someone in jail. It only lasts while you're inside. And in the end, you want to get out. You do. You want your freedom. I don't even know what happened to him. I hoped he'd see one of my movies and write to me, but maybe he just wanted to forget."

I told her about Christine's and James Baldwin's admiration of her. "Negroes seem able to identify with you; yet, as a blonde star, you're a white symbol."

She was impatient with that. "I don't want to be a symbol of anything. Negroes can sometimes see through appearances better than whites. Blondes don't even appeal to some of them. I'm not a sex symbol, but busty Miss Anne," and she laughed merrily, her bust rising beneath her blouse. "Gee," she said, "we *are* talking seriously. I thought this was to be a drunken party."

"Let's get drunk then." I brought her another drink from the bar.

"I read your article about me," she said. "Who's Mrs. Patrick Campbell?"

I had described her in the article as a cross between a theatrical grandame like Mrs. Campbell and a child star like Shirley Temple.

She beamed when I told her, but she added that she took a dim view of being even remotely compared to "Lolita Temple."

"Sorry. Now that I know you better, I wouldn't compare you to anyone."

"All is forgiven. Do you enjoy interviewing?"

"Only if I learn what the person is really like."

"Do you ever do that? I mean, aren't most interviews too short? And don't people play roles?"

"Sometimes one catches a glimpse of the truth."

"I must be careful," she said.

"You're safe. We've agreed I won't write anything."

"And you keep your agreements?"

"A reporter has to."

"Okay," she said, as if she were satisfied. "What are you reading at present?"

It was my turn to laugh. It reminded me of an English joke. When there was an uneasy silence between strangers, one always asked: "Have you read any good books recently?" I explained it to her.

"But I'm serious."

"I recently read Norman Mailer's *The Deer Park*. It might interest you. It's about Hollywood. I'll get you a copy."

"Do you ever feel some books are beyond you? I mean, your mind can't handle them?"

"Yes, particularly certain philosophical works in translation. It's almost like a foreign language though the words are English."

"It makes me feel so dumb sometimes."

"I wouldn't worry about it if I were you. You have sharper instincts than many intellectuals. You don't want to blunt your instincts just for the sake of secondhand knowledge. I'd rather be beautiful than wise."

She frowned, and I felt as if I'd made a bad error. "That sounds like Sir Olivier telling me to be sexy. I'd rather be wise. I wish I'd had a longer formal education. Sometimes when Arthur and his friends were talking, I couldn't follow. I don't know much about politics. I'm just past the goodies and baddies stage. The politicians get away with murder because most Americans don't know any more about it than I do. Less even. Arthur was always very good at explaining, but I felt at my age I should have known. It's my country and I should know what they're doing with it." She sat up. "What time is it?"

I stood up and looked at the bar clock. It was after six.

"I must go. I'm going out to dinner with some friends. Want to come?"

"I've got a dinner date."

"I hope it's not with a girl," she said severely. "You must

131

be loyal to Christine. Many American men are very disloyal and yet they expect their women to be loyal to them."

"I've just had a drink with the world's sex symbol. Christine might not think that was loyal."

"We're just friends," she said as if she were speaking to reporters. She laughed and got up. "I must fly. I'll be very late. But people expect that. Some friends give me the time an hour early so I'll arrive on time. You don't need to come out with me."

"I'll see you to a cab."

I hoped she wouldn't be recognized going out. I didn't feel like acting as her bodyguard. But she was very cool. It was a familiar situation for her and she could turn the magnet on or off. Now it was off. One's eyes automatically followed her rear, but there was no wiggle or waggle in her walk. Several men stared, but no one called out after her.

"Have you time for me to find a bookstore and get you *The Deer Park?*"

"If you want to," she said obligingly.

We walked a few blocks along Eighth Avenue. People were still going home, rushing toward the subway or the Port Authority Bus Terminal, and she blended easily with the crowd, without fuss or seeking attention. Most people were in such a hurry that they didn't even glance at us. A middle-aged wino with a black, ravaged face stopped us for a quarter. She gave him one and he thanked her very courteously. I hurried her on.

"I should have given him a dollar," she said, looking back with concern. "I wasn't thinking."

"He was pleased anyway."

But she wasn't satisfied until she went back and gave the man a dollar. He couldn't have been more surprised if a gold brick had fallen out of the sky. She smiled shyly at him, embarrassed.

Such actions are not missed on Eighth Avenue. We hadn't gone far before a flower-seller waylaid us, an old woman with a solid, cheery Irish face. I bought Marilyn a red rose and she stuck it in her head scarf so that the rose came over the right side of her head.

"That looks pretty," the old woman said, peering at Marilyn. "Don't I know your face, darlin'?" Oh, I thought, here it comes. I watched recognition slowly dawn. "Aren't you Marilyn Monroe?"

Marilyn nodded, smiling.

"How're you doin', darlin'?" the woman asked, squeezing her hand.

"Pretty well," Marilyn said, giving the old woman her whole attention. "How're you doin', yourself?"

"Can't complain, Marilyn dear. Sorry you and your old man split up. You have as bad luck with men as I do. Better luck next time. Keep smilin', darlin'."

Marilyn smiled. "Good luck, flower lady."

But it wasn't so easy to escape. The old woman wanted an autograph, but she had no paper. I tore a page out of my notebook. Marilyn asked her her name and wrote her a good luck message and signed it. The old woman beamed. "That's luvly, Marilyn."

We walked quickly away as the old woman looked around for someone to tell. News that Marilyn Monroe was there would soon be all over Eighth Avenue.

We found a paperback bookstore and I bought her *The Deer Park*.

"I'll read it," she said, "and I'll tell you what I think of it."

I stopped a cab for her. The driver had an alert, knowing face, and I bet he would recognize her before he got her home. Her disguise wasn't all that good.

She said through the open window: "Let's do this again. It was fun. I enjoyed it."

"I did, too," I said. "Are you being polite or serious?"

"Serious."

"When then?"

"Day after tomorrow." She added apologetically, "I've got business all day tomorrow."

We made a date for the same bar. She said she liked it.

I waved her off and then went in a snack bar to make some notes of our conversation. In those days of constant heavy-weight interviewing, I had a good, practiced memory for conversations, so I remembered what Marilyn had said even if I didn't perhaps always remember her exact words. I still wondered if she was just being friendly or whether she had a purpose behind it all. But what purpose could she have? If I wasn't writing anything, I was of no use to her career. Suspicion still lingered like poison.

16

I found myself looking forward to the day after tomorrow in a way I didn't like. Surely I wasn't going to become obsessed with Marilyn. There was no future in that. I phoned Christine in New Orleans. The situation there was quietening down. The city would have to accept integration sooner or later; there was no going back. When I said I'd seen Marilyn, Christine was as interested as a fan-club member. "She sounds like fun." It was her highest praise about a white person, and it was true. The casual couple of drinks had been fun. Marilyn could transform a simple bar—and you, too—with her determination to have a good time. I think that was why she influenced so many sad, insecure people who sensed this quality in her when they saw her movies. It was a common experience in New York to see someone resembling her. From the back, it looked like her image, even to the sexy walk. But when I crossed the street to take a closer look, a strange face always regarded me from under the blonde hair. She was an imitation Marilyn, one of many who saw their ideal self in her.

I met Paula Strasberg and had a pleasant chat. A quick, small, plump woman with bright eyes and a jolly laugh, she seemed more at home in New York than in Reno or Hollywood. But the bright eyes grew cold and the jolly laugh died when I asked clumsily if there was any danger that the Method might make Marilyn too introspective.

"What gave you that idea?" she asked in a hard, cold voice.

I realized I had made a mistake. I wasn't going to learn anything and tried unsuccessfully to get out of it. "Some of the sessions at the studio suggested it. Students examine themselves so closely that they don't project much."

"Actors should know themselves and their craft," she said. "There are too many unthinking, automatic performances. People patronize Marilyn. They think she's weak in the head and in her character. They don't know her. She's very intelligent and sensitive and a fast learner. She is never satisfied. She examines everything she does. Are you trying to tell me such intelligent behavior is wrong? If so, you're as bad as those moronic people in Hollywood who underrated her for years."

"No, no, I didn't mean—"

"Then what did you mean?" She was behaving a little like her husband in a session at the studio, when a student seemed to miss the point and had to be brought to his senses with a shaft of sarcasm.

"She seems at her best when she doesn't worry about a role but just plays—"

Paula Strasberg interrupted with a scoffing laugh. "You see the performance. You don't see what lies behind it. It is like the iceberg—a great deal lies unseen, all the thoughts and the work in conveying the thoughts. What is a character without a complete psychology? The actor has to express that psychology in behavior on the stage. What the author provides is just the tip of the iceberg. You have to find in yourself all that lies under the surface. I went out to Reno with Marilyn to help her do that, and I worked out her problems for her."

She made Marilyn seem very dependent. I wondered how Marilyn would react to what she'd said. Marilyn had a history of these close teacher-student relationships, but in time she always seemed to break them off. Would the Strasbergs be any different?

She didn't seem to like it much when I said I'd had a drink with Marilyn.

"I hope you didn't tell her your silly idea."

"It was just a chat."

"You're not going to write anything?"

"No, no."

"Someday you should write a long, serious study of Marilyn as an actress. She's going to be one of the great ones. I'll talk to you then. Tell you what it means. Too introspective? Oh, no—"

I said I'd probably exaggerated the difficulty of successful collaborations from watching Miller and Huston on *The Misfits.*

She made a face. Neither name seemed to please her. "Impossible," she said. "Quite impossible from the beginning. Marilyn and I were in the middle. But ours is not a collaboration. Marilyn is a student of ours. Our greatest. Almost one of the family. I know her as well as my own daughter. I know her problems, her worries. I can help her to overcome them. . . ."

She seemed to have forgiven me for my slip. She even invited me to her next New Year's Eve party, which she said was always one of the big theatrical events of the year, and she gave her jolly laugh again.

17

She arrived in a different mood, coming into the bar this time very tentatively and nervously, nearly an hour late. She stood uneasily near the bar, looking around, and I rushed to meet her. She was dressed in the same sloppy way. Because of her nervousness, she seemed even less like the famous star.

"I'm late," she said as if I might scold her.

I got her a drink. A gin and tonic, I think. Her manner seemed rather distant when I joined her at the table and I wondered if she'd had a lot to drink already. Maybe it was pills.

"I nearly didn't come," she said.

"I'm glad you did."

"I felt like staying inside—away from people."

"You got the blues?"

"Sort of." She took a quick drink. "I saw Monty Clift. That man is beautiful, but he's killing himself slowly." She laughed nervously. "Or not so slowly."

"I heard he'd been seen in the bathhouses."

"What does he need that for? He's sort of running away from himself." She grinned. "I know the feeling." She burrowed in her bag and brought out the copy of *The Deer Park* I'd given her and pushed it across the table. "He's too impressed by power, in my opinion."

"I thought he understood it."

"You can't fool me about that," she said. "I've felt that way myself—scared of being a loser." And to back it up, she told me again the story about Betty Grable she'd told me in

143

Reno. "They won't ever humiliate me that way. I'm going into the theater or character acting—or I'm just *going*. I'll never wait for them to say 'so long.' I've had fame, but maybe I can learn to live without it. What do you think?"

"I'm sure you could. It might even have its advantages. Personal relationships must be easier."

"You don't attract so many heels. Sometimes I've got such lousy taste in men. There was a whole period when I felt flattered if a man took an interest in me—any man! I believed too easily in people, and then I went on believing in them even after they disappointed me over and over again. I must have been very stupid in those days. I guess I'm capable of doing it again with some guy, only he'd have to be someone more outstanding than a heel. Not that I didn't pay for it all—all I've ever done. There were times when I'd be with one of my husbands and I'd run into one of these Hollywood heels at a party and they'd paw me cheaply in front of everybody as if they were saying, *Oh, we had her.* I guess it's the classic situation of an ex-whore, though I was never a whore in that sense. I was never kept; I always kept myself. But there was a period when I responded too much to flattery and slept around too much, thinking it would help my career, though I always liked the guy at the time. They were always so full of self-confidence and I had none at all and they made me feel better. But you don't get self-confidence that way. You have to get it by earning respect. I've never given up on anyone who I thought respected me." Her eyes were wide and her gaze direct, as if she were appealing to be believed.

"I'm sure you've been respected far more than you realize."

"Do you really think so?"

"People respect you because they feel you've survived

hard times and endured, and although you've become famous, you haven't become phony."

"Thank you," she said. "I've certainly tried." She sat back and relaxed a little. "You must excuse me if I'm not good company. I've been having trouble sleeping. It makes me grumpy. I used to have a bad temper, but I try to control it nowadays. Poor Arthur, he saw some of it. Flashes of lightning and thunder! That's why I try and be sweet, but sometimes it's not possible."

I told her about my meeting with Paula Strasberg. "She and Lee Strasberg really believe you're going to be a great stage actress."

"Oh, I hope. I'm working very hard to be good enough to have the confidence. Their belief in me helps me to keep going, especially when I'm not sleeping and haven't much energy. They work so hard with me on the essentials—like a pianist and his scales. Projection, movement, breath control— all those things. And I'm doing short scenes like I did with Mr. Chekhov. I read once the role of Blanche Du Bois in Tennessee Williams' *A Streetcar Named Desire*. I'd like to play that on Broadway when I'm older. I like the last line so much. She says —I forget the exact words—something about she's always had to depend on strangers for kindness. I know what she meant. Friends and relatives can let you down. You can depend on them too much. But don't depend *too* much on strangers, honey. Some strangers gave me a hard time when I was a kid."

"I read once that you were raped as a child."

"Don't let's talk about that. I'm tired of talking about that. I'm sorry I ever mentioned it to anyone." She absent-mindedly wiped the table with a paper napkin and then grinned at herself. "The housewife. I enjoy housework. Takes my mind off things. But thinking of what Blanche said, do you

145

know who I've always depended on? Not strangers, not friends. The telephone! That's my best friend. I seldom write letters, but I love calling friends, especially late at night when I can't sleep. I have this dream we all get up and go out to a drugstore."

"Schwab's?"

"No, that scene sort of depresses me." She played with her drink, thinking. "I was remembering Monty Clift. People who aren't fit to open the door for him sneer at his homosexuality. What do they know about it? Labels—people love putting labels on each other. Then they feel safe. People tried to make me into a lesbian. I laughed. No sex is wrong if there's love in it. But too often people act like it's gymnasium work, mechanical. They'd be as satisfied with a machine from a drugstore as with another human being. I sometimes felt they were trying to make me into a machine." She smiled with what looked like embarrassment and took a sip of her drink. But she didn't let go of the subject. It was as if there was something bugging her. She might have been talking to herself as she went on.

"I sometimes felt I was hooked on sex, the way an alcoholic is on liquor or a junkie on dope. My body turned all these people on, like turning on an electric light, and there was so rarely anything human in it. Marilyn Monroe became a burden, a—what do you call it?—an albatross. People expected so much of me, I sometimes hated them. It was too much of a strain. I still feel that way. Marilyn Monroe has to look a certain way—be *beautiful*—and act a certain way, be talented. I wondered if I could live up to their expectations. There were times on *The Misfits*, in those emotional scenes, when I had a feeling I'd fail however hard I'd try, and I didn't want to go to the set in the morning. I was sorry then I wasn't a waitress or a cleaning lady and free of people's great demands. Sometimes it would be a big relief to be no longer famous. But we actors and actresses are such worriers, such—what is your word?—Narcissus types. I sit in front of the mirror for hours looking for signs of age. Yet I like old people; they have great qualities younger people don't have. I want to grow old without face-lifts. They take the life out of a face, the character. I want to have the courage to be loyal to the face I've made. Sometimes I think it would be easier to avoid old age, to die young, but then you'd never complete your life, would you? You'd never wholly know yourself."

"Lots of people don't want to know themselves."

"I don't think I'm like that," she said seriously. "But sometimes I get scared of finding out. For a long time I was scared I'd find out that I was like my mother and end up in the crazy house. I wonder when I break down if I'm not tough enough—like her. But I'm hoping to get stronger." Her spirits seemed to rise. "I ask myself what am I afraid of. I know I have talent. I know I can act. Well, get on with it, Marilyn. I feel I still try to ingratiate myself with people, try to tell them what they want to hear. That's fear, too. We should all start to live before we get too old. Fear is stupid. So are regrets. You know, for years I had this big regret that I hadn't gotten a high school diploma. What does it matter now? All those high school diploma-holders would love to be movie stars. You've got to keep your sense of proportion. I guess that diploma kinda represents for me a home, a security I never really had. I was never used to being happy. For years I thought having a father and being married meant happiness. I've never had a father— you can't *buy* them!—but I've been married three times and haven't found permanent happiness yet. You've got to get the most out of the moment. Let's make some mischief." She laughed and looked around the bar. Suddenly she was gay, as though she'd come out on the other side of some confused, unhappy mood.

"Would you like to dance on the bar?" I asked, trying to match her new mood and feeling the obviousness of my attempt. But she wasn't the kind of person who wanted you to succeed every time; she gave you marks for trying.

"We'd only be thrown out," she said gleefully. She made me feel like I had made a good joke. "This is a men's bar. Women have to lie low."

Not Marilyn Monroe, I thought. She could take it over and have all the tough guys at the bar eating out of her hand. But she looked shy then, as if asserting herself was the last thing she had in mind. Fear of rejection seemed to be more in her thoughts.

"What would Mae West do?" she said, chuckling.

"Probably wrestle the bartender."

"I learned a few tricks from her—that impression of laughing at, or mocking, her own sexuality."

"You are a *beautiful* Mae West!"

"She's a handsome woman." In an accurate Mae West voice she said: "Come up and see me sometime." She pushed her glass away. "You know what I'd like? A cup of coffee."

"There's a snack bar next door." She began to get up. "No, wait here. I'll bring you one." She'd be much more visible in a well-lit snack bar, and I wanted her to myself a little longer.

She was dabbing at her nose when I returned with a container of coffee.

"Does my nose look kinda shiny?"

"No, it looks fine."

"You're a great help." She gulped some coffee. "I hope the bartender won't object to me drinking coffee from outside."

148

"He's too busy to notice. But if he comes over, just flash him a smile."

"You think that would work?" She gave a glassy mechanical smile.

"Put a little more love into it."

She laughed. She was in a strange mood, all right.

"You know, I've been thinking of writing my will. Can't tell you why, but it's been on my mind. It's made me feel sort of gloomy. I always thought you did that when you were old or sick, but people tell me everyone oughta make a will if you've got something to leave. Saves a lot of trouble. I haven't got any fortune now, but maybe I'll make something out of *The Misfits*. Anyway it's on my mind. Without a will, everything'd go to my mother, I guess, and what would she do with it?"

"Have you seen the complete film of *The Misfits?*"

"I'm still too close to it. Some people say it's pretty good. I wonder what the critics will say." She sounded anxious.

"They'll praise your performance."

"Oh, I hope. I wish Clark were still alive to see it. I felt guilty when he died, in case I'd put too much strain on him while we were making the movie. But that was stupid. He had a bad heart. No one can give you that. But he was such a strong, upright man—a real gentleman—that it was a great shock. Like your father dying. I wept all night. I'd have gone to his funeral, but I was afraid of breaking down. I loved that man. I wish we could have met when we were both young and about the same age, but I guess it probably wouldn't have worked out. When you're both famous, it's a double problem—even when you're famous in different ways, like Arthur and I were."

Her eyes widened, as though she couldn't quite believe what she was thinking. "Fame causes such envy. People hate you sometimes just because you're famous. They're phony to

149

your face. See you around—like never. I like to be accepted for my own sake, but a lot of people don't care who you *are.* All they're interested in is your fame—while you've got it. I like to escape it, like we're doing now. When I was a kid, the world often seemed a pretty grim place. I loved to escape through games and make-believe. You can do that even better as an actress, but sometimes it seems you escape altogether and people never let you come back. You're trapped in your fame. Maybe I'll never get out of it now until it's over. Fame has gone and I'm old. What should I do then? I don't think it'll throw me. I have ideas. I'll be interested in *everything.* Character acting, poetry reading, yoga, travel—everything. That's the way to stay alive. It is," she said, laughing self-consciously.

She finished her coffee. Silence.

"Balzac was the world's greatest coffee-drinker," I said to break the silence.

"The French writer?" Again that uncertain look.

"He wrote from late at night until the next day on thick black coffee, to keep himself awake."

"Didn't he ever sleep?"

"If you read his biography, it's hard to see how he had the time. He died when he was fifty, worn out."

"I wonder how I'll feel when I'm fifty. Half a century!"

"You'll probably feel completely at peace with yourself."

"I hope so. When's your birthday?"

"January 8."

"What's your sign?"

"Capricorn."

"The goat!"

"What's yours?"

"Gemini."

"What kind of people are Geminis?"

"Jekyll and Hyde. Two in one."

"And that's you?"

"More than two. I'm so many people. They shock me sometimes. I wish I was just *me!* I used to think maybe I was going crazy, until I discovered some people I admired were like that, too. Arthur's about seven hundred different people." She laughed, looking a little embarrassed. Suddenly she was off in another direction. She was a restless conversationalist. "Do people ever get over being shy? I think it's with you for life—like the color of your eyes."

"Maybe inside. You can learn to handle it outside, hide it. You've learned to do it, right?"

"Not always. Sometimes I *freeze.*" She looked very serious. "I could have got so much more done if I had more self-confidence."

I told her what Tennessee Williams had told me, that he had no self-confidence about his work. Her remark about escaping from the world also reminded me of what he had said about escaping through his writing. "You two sound alike."

"Maybe too much alike—like me and Monty Clift. You don't look for someone like yourself. You look for someone different, with different qualities. Nobody could be more unlike the men I've been friendly with—Arthur and Joe and Frank and . . . and, and, and. So many, yet here I am alone. I don't like being alone. Nobody does. It puts too many pressures on you. But sometimes it keeps you out of trouble."

"It can also get you *into* trouble."

"How?"

"You want company, so you choose any company, which sometimes means bad company."

"Yes, that's true. I've done that. I must be careful now not to do it again. I've been with some stinkers."

"Everybody has." My remark sounded feeble, but she made me want to say something to help, and I didn't know what.

"Even the stinkers go with stinkers." That amused her, and she sat back and laughed. Wanting the mood to change, she was trying to force herself to feel gay.

I told her the old story about Harold Ross, the founder-editor of *The New Yorker* magazine, when someone complained that the women in James Thurber's drawings had no sex appeal. "They do for Thurber's men," he is supposed to have replied.

"You mean stinkers aren't stinkers to stinkers," she said very seriously, as though trying to work out a complicated mathematical equation.

"I guess they're not."

"It all depends on where you're coming from."

"What you're standing on."

"What you are," she said.

A friend of hers had told me: "Conversations with Marilyn are apt to get suddenly serious and go anywhere." I could see what she meant. I felt bad about not being able to keep her in a gay mood when she was trying so hard to raise her spirits, but maybe it wasn't my fault.

She watched a grey cat walk lazily across the top of the bar. "If that was a rat, they'd all run for cover—"

"Or try to kill it. A rat's dangerous."

"Someone told me they're only dangerous if you attack them first."

"Don't believe it."

"A cat can be dangerous, too."

"Not many. They're exceptions. Cats leave you alone."

"Depends where they are." She suddenly laughed. "I'm

going out on a limb. Have you ever noticed how you can talk yourself into saying impossible things?"

"I used to report what politicians said. They're always saying impossible things."

"John Kennedy talks sense," she said firmly.

"Not all the time."

"Oh, he does."

"Did you see where he's made his brother, Bobby, attorney general?"

She looked surprised. Her knowledge of current events seemed to be spotty. "Keeping it in the family, huh? How many Kennedys are there? Maybe he'll give them all jobs and it'll be a Kennedy government." She laughed. "They say their father made them all millionaires."

"You sound respectful."

"I admire their zest, the impression they give of enjoying life. It's so rare in our public life. Public figures generally seem like stuffed shirts or tombstones—monuments. If you don't enjoy life, you're wasting your time here, but so many of us make that mistake."

"I think that's one reason you're so popular with moviegoers: you seem to be enjoying yourself."

That pleased her. "You really think so?"

"They also identify with you as Cinderella."

"Cinderella? That's as bad as Lolita Temple."

"I mean the beautiful poor girl who has overcome."

"I haven't overcome. I wish I had!"

"To moviegoers, you have. You're a star!"

"Whatever that means, however much it's worth." She looked wistful for a moment and then smiled, gay again. "But don't knock it. It can set you free. Where would I be without it? On a calendar—nude." She grinned. "How shocked some of the studio people were at the time, and now it seems like nothing. I enjoyed doing it. I'm on close terms with my body because I look after it. I don't mistreat it. But sometimes I feel infatuated by it. I'm too much into it then. When the photographers come, it's like looking in a mirror. They think they arrange me to suit themselves, but I use them to put over myself. It's necessary in the movie business, but I often hate it. I never show it, though. It could ruin me. I need their goodwill. I'm not stupid. Even Arthur used to go over the pictures, helping me spot the bad ones. Of course, the bad ones were those that didn't make me seem beautiful." She giggled at that.

"I felt occasionally that I was killing the truth when I killed the ones that were bad for my public image. Here is Marilyn Monroe with egg on her face. I used to feel as tied to the beauty business as an addict to his drugs. It's a relief to get in sloppy clothes and not worry about the impression you're making—about any of it. But it's part of my career—my life! —and I accept it. When my looks start to go, so will most of the fans. *So long, it's been nice knowing you.* But I won't care. I'll be ready. There's other kinds of beauty, other ways of impressing people and getting over. I hope to do it by sheer acting. I *do,*" she added, as if I were going to challenge it— or laugh. "You can go on forever in the theater. The distance, the footlights, the makeup—it all helps create whatever illusion you wish. Who was that great actress you compared me to?"

"Shirley Temple?"

She gave a mock snarl.

"Mrs. Patrick Campbell."

"Mrs. Marilyn Monroe. How does that sound?" She was working herself up into a merry mood again. It seemed like a constant struggle that day not to lapse into sadness. She also seemed obsessed with the idea of the theater as her salvation. It was something she was clutching at, but I wondered how substantial it would be if she had nothing else left. I kept seeing her arriving an hour late, or in the ninetieth performance, forgetting her lines in a crucial scene, and then her agonized look of breakdown. All actors and actresses, I thought, when they stare so much at themselves, must stare also at all their bad dreams. They have to have great strength to live so closely with such dreams. Marilyn Monroe was undoubtedly a tough professional in many ways, but she also seemed frail and vulnerable. How much of this side of her was an act for sympathy, a part of the seduction scene?

I still didn't know the answer, but as if to remind me of it, she leaned over and stroked the bar cat which had finished inspecting the regulars at the bar and had come down to sniff us. "I wonder if he's an alcoholic," she said. "He's very skinny. They probably feed him liquor instead of food." The cat purred under her careful stroking. "I think he's a bit high now." She mumbled something to the cat that sounded like "mumblebumbledee." The cat didn't seem very interested. "I asked him in cat language what his favorite drink was."

"What did he say?"

"Milk—but he doesn't get much. It's harder to get here than Scotch whiskey!"

"Poor cat."

"He's not *poor*. He's tough. You shouldn't pity animals. It's superior. We're all poor."

"I'm sorry. I meant to be sympathetic."

"Well"—she smiled—"We can't love everyone, I guess. I've done my share of trying." Suddenly she looked sad again.

155

The gay mood was over. She stopped stroking the cat. "Time to go," she said. "I'm hours late already." I felt she was just getting away to be by herself so she wouldn't have to make so much of an effort. For some reason I didn't know, it was a bad day for her.

The next time I went to the Actors Studio, she wasn't there. At least I couldn't see her. She could have crept in after the session started and stayed at the back, but I kept glancing round and at the end got up quickly and walked to the door and surveyed the crowd; but I saw no Marilyn.

My notes here are a little confusing, but I think it was at this session that I watched Franchot Tone introduce his son to Lee Strasberg. I had seen Franchot Tone star in movies since I was a boy—a tall, slim man with fine bones and a memorable, light-comedy style. He was older and heavier now in the flesh, worn and apparently nervous, but still recognizable and famous, though his days of being a great star were over. He and Lee Strasberg had been colleagues in the old days in the Group Theater, and I expected to see them greet each other with enthusiasm, like old friends. But Tone hovered uncertainly near Strasberg's entourage and introduced his handsome, teenage son tentatively, as if unsure of his reception. Strasberg never seemed to have an easy manner with people, and he treated Tone rather sharply and condescendingly, with a guarded, shy abruptness unlike the self-consciously hearty manner with which he greeted other visiting celebrities. Perhaps some ancient rancor lay between them; perhaps Tone wanted to enroll his son in the studio and Strasberg thought he wasn't ready and was embarrassed about it. But Strasberg didn't seem so easily embarrassed. I had seen him ruthlessly criticize students who had done scenes after insufficient preparation. Tone

159

was an old colleague; surely Strasberg could be frank with him. Perhaps Tone was the one who felt embarrassed; he certainly appeared the more uneasy, and he was usually a poised man.

I wondered why Strasberg appeared to be so gentle with Marilyn Monroe and so offhand with Tone. She, of course, needed gentle handling, and no doubt she had charmed him. She was certainly a great recruit for the studio in terms of publicity, but there was more to it than that. I felt that here was a key to Marilyn, and so I kept worrying over it.

Strasberg had committed himself and his wife personally as well as professionally, a rare concession for such an aloof teacher. And she apparently had committed herself. Yet if you could believe the Marilyn-watchers over the years, she had a history of drawing what she needed from people and then cutting herself off from them. Perhaps, if she sensed any over-dependence, any personal psychological danger, she would cut herself off from the Strasbergs and the studio as she recently had from Arthur Miller, on whom she had once depended far more than she now did on Lee Strasberg. But she generally explained such changes another way. People she had trusted—such as her ex-husbands—had eventually "disappointed" her.

When I left the studio that day I still couldn't see her among the students. We were supposed to meet the next day and I wondered if she'd show up. I imagined her going through some crisis—unable to sleep, filling up on pills to the point of suffocation. Such scenes were easy to imagine after *The Misfits*. No insurance company or backer would ever again feel entirely safe with her.

By chance I met a movie critic who had seen the completed *Misfits*. I asked him if it was going to be a great success. He stared absentmindedly up the block on Broadway. "It's like a European movie," he said at last.

"But most of them show only in the art houses."

"That's what I mean. It's a slice of life. I expected to see people go to the bathroom. You need more plot for popular entertainment."

"And Marilyn?"

He was slow to reply. "No easy answer," he said. "Her best and her worst. She aims higher, achieves more. But sometimes you see the strain, you see her *trying*. You see all the Strasberg lessons going through her head."

It wasn't good news. *The Misfits* wasn't going to make the critics finally take her seriously as a great dramatic actress. Marilyn hadn't gotten there yet. Unfortunately she had gambled greatly on this movie—maybe all she had left. And with her knowledge of the movie business and her native shrewdness, the news would already have reached her and have been assessed. Maybe that was why she had had a bad day and hadn't come to the studio.

I waited an hour for her. After the first few minutes I was convinced she wouldn't come, but I went on waiting. She had made the appointment, but what other reason was there for her to keep it if she was in trouble? I wasn't a close friend, a relative, or a psychiatrist. I couldn't bring her much comfort. I was merely related to her professional life. After an hour, greatly disappointed, feeling that this was the end of our acquaintance and our meetings, I left the bar and wandered down Eighth Avenue, back to where I was staying.

Tennessee Williams had asked me where that was, and when I told him the YMCA on West 34th Street, known as William Sloane House, he recalled that he had stayed there when he first came to New York and worked at night as a movie usher on 42nd Street, among the hustlers and winos and homeless who slept in the moviehouses. I was staying there to save money, so I could remain in New York as long as possible. I had received a $1,000 travel award from the English-Speaking Union and it was fast running out.

You had to show your key before you could enter the elevator, and the toilets and showers were down the hall. I had just reached my room when the phone rang. A slightly breathless voice said, "Apologies, apologies, apologies. I was sleeping. I took some pills. Will you forgive me?"

I'd forgotten I'd told her where I was staying.

"Can we still meet?" she said. "Or are you too tired?"

No, indeed.

165

Fifteen minutes later we were sitting over a drink. She had on makeup and was very lively at first. I felt she was giving a performance to hide her real feelings. I wished she trusted me enough not to bother. But maybe she was afraid of breaking down. Or perhaps it was part of her pride to try to be cheerful with other people. I brushed aside her continued apologies with some remark about her being worth waiting for and she joshed me about English politeness, with some reference to Sir Olivier. Somehow Yves Montand's name came up, and she asked me if I'd ever interviewed him. I told her no, but I'd met his wife, Simone Signoret.

"They certainly seem to have an understanding. He can flirt and then go back. I've always thought of marriage. . . . Well, when I was interested in it, in my husband, I wasn't interested in anyone else. I don't see how a marriage can last if you run around. . . ."

If she wasn't fantasizing, she had a touching view of marriage. Strangely puritanical and old-fashioned by Hollywood standards, with the stress on complete loyalty. How badly she would take the least betrayal! I remembered Huston's story in Ireland of how the truth had broken up a marriage. If she had had an affair with Montand, as the gossip columnists suggested, it meant she was betraying Miller, by her own standards. But perhaps the marriage was already over by then and she was merely repaying Miller for some act of betrayal she held against him.

What a strange contrast Signoret and Monroe must have presented. Signoret, with her passionate interest in politics, was such a sophisticated Frenchwoman. Many of Marilyn's attitudes would have seemed naive to her. And yet the two women shared an earthiness, a directness, a refusal to play the big star. Neither was a phony. But Signoret's French sophistication, her

166

acceptance of what life was like, would protect her from despair in a way that Marilyn would never know. Marilyn often seemed defenseless, even though part of it was deliberate. Signoret's attitude toward acting was also quite different. She certainly wouldn't have enrolled with Strasberg. She told me she didn't "build a part." She knew she should be aware of everything in a role, "but a lot is instinct." She was quite relaxed about it. Acting was a job. A role had to be "in you." You had to be cast accurately. But instinct played a large part in the actual performance.

Marilyn didn't like that, and so rationalized. Signoret wasn't "ambitious enough" as an actress. To get her off the subject, I told her what John Steinbeck had said to me about Hollywood. When he was very poor, someone had offered to try to get him a job in Hollywood. Steinbeck said he didn't want one. "Fine," the man said. "Now I'm sure I can get you one." Steinbeck said to me: "Needing something badly is a sure way of not getting it. If you don't want it, you'll get it. I used to apply for all the literary prizes and I never got any until I didn't need them any longer."

"That's the story of my life," she said. "Being a movie actress was never as much fun as dreaming of being one. When I'd nearly given up, I got a break. Then when I didn't want the studio kind of star roles, I was showered with them. The same kind of thing can happen in personal relations. When you don't want a lover, all kinds of opportunities come your way."

She said Steinbeck was a friend of Arthur Miller's and asked me what I thought of him. What could I say? Steinbeck had been a hero of my boyhood. I told her about his fear of popularity. "It's a murderous thing," he'd told me, "because it creates a self-consciousness which makes it difficult to work without getting away from people. It also creates a self-consciousness in other people toward you, so that they are no longer themselves. They become actors and characters and react as characters rather than as they normally would. That loss of anonymity is a terrible thing—"

"But if I hadn't become popular," she said. "I'd still be a Hollywood slave. Nobody made me except the people. My popularity with them set me free."

"I guess Steinbeck was thinking of writers."

"Yes, Arthur found it very difficult to work under the spotlight. But in a way, not being used to it, I think he enjoyed it."

Mindful of what some critics might say about *The Misfits*, I told her what Steinbeck had said about one critic. "He was the meanest son of a bitch that ever lived. His criticism was a hatchet job on every book. Then he had a book published and his whole attitude changed. He became benign and helpful. We had another critic who was forty years a bachelor. Then he got married, and he changed, too." Steinbeck told me: "I don't have any positive quarrel with critics. I just hate them. They confuse me so."

Marilyn laughed; she enjoyed that. "Who was the critic who was the meanest son of a bitch that ever lived?"

"He didn't say."

"Or you won't say. That's what I like about you. You know how to keep a secret."

I didn't like to take credit where it wasn't due—Steinbeck *hadn't* named the critic—but it wasn't worth arguing about, and I didn't mind her having a good opinion of me!

"I've sometimes tried to charm critics, give them the impression I'm really attracted to them, and it works. With journalists and photographers generally. Experienced as they are, they're not beyond being wooed." She looked mischievous.

"Is that your technique with me?"

She shook her head. "We're just talking."

She asked me about Steinbeck's books and then said she'd been reading Scott Fitzgerald's last, unfinished novel, *The Last Tycoon*, which she'd found an artful view of Hollywood but too romantic. "He's missed out on the truly violent gangster element. The mob. Even his bastards seemed sort of civilized."

I asked her if she'd read Steinbeck's *East of Eden*. I was very fond of the character Tom in the novel. Steinbeck told me that Tom had been based on his uncle and that he had named his son after him. "He was a fine man"—a fine man who had committed suicide eventually. At the mention of suicide, she seemed to draw back in her seat.

"Why did he do it?"

"He was too sensitive and blamed himself—"

"I understand," she said, cutting me short. "I tried it once and I was kinda disappointed it didn't work." She laughed. "No more worries."

"You seem too full of life."

"You oughta've seen me this morning. I saw the dawn in. I couldn't sleep. Sometimes nothing works, not even the pills."

"Maybe you need more fresh air and exercise, more relaxing."

"I'm just naturally a poor sleeper. But you're right. I miss the country."

"I thought you'd get lots of weekend invitations."

"Not many I want to accept. Sometimes I'm on my own a lot. I could go places, but I don't feel like it."

"Are you looking forward to getting back to movie work?" I began to sound like an interviewer again.

"I'd like to make a good comedy again. We may do Somerset Maugham's *Rain* on television."

"With John Gielgud as the minister? We talked about it in Reno, remember?"

"Maybe Sir Olivier was enough Englishman for me."

"Gielgud has a lot of prestige."

Suddenly she was annoyed. How had she interpreted my casual remark—that I was suggesting that she hadn't a lot of prestige as a serious actress? Olivier must have received such a glare when he asked her to be "sexy." I tried to recover from my error.

"But he's not a Method actor," I said quietly, as if I'd made a simple blunder. Smile from me, no response from her.

"I'm sorry," I said. "Did I hurt your feelings?"

She shook her head. "I was just thinking. . . ." She went into a long silence. I wondered if she was doped up and not functioning properly. She didn't want any liquor.

"Marilyn," I said.

She started, as if she were coming back from somewhere. She worried me a little. What should I do if I found myself with a sick Monroe on my hands? I didn't know her address except that it was somewhere on East 57th Street. She had talked of inviting me over, but I hadn't followed it up. I preferred the bar meetings, when I had her to myself without an entourage of hangers-on.

"I'm sorry," she said. "Today is blue Friday."

"Why?" Was I inviting trouble by asking?

"Sometimes I feel I make all these plans for nothing. Maybe I can't carry them out. Maybe I haven't got what it takes." She suddenly looked so depressed that I felt sorry for her.

"I don't believe it. You're so talented—"

"You need more than talent. Sometimes I feel so low on energy."

"Energy is a big part of talent. You're just feeling bad."

"Why am I boring you with my blues?" She sat up straighter, smiling, determined to be cheerful. "Tell me about your girl in New Orleans. I hope you're being faithful to her."

As her mood seemed to change for the better, mine changed for the worse. Here was the famous movie star getting no fun out of her fame or money. What could I say? I searched desperately for jokes or diversions, and the more I did, the more depressed I became.

Mention of Christine got her going on the civil rights campaign in the South. "We ought to do more to help Martin Luther King. Have you ever interviewed him?"

I told her how depressed I had once found King in Atlanta. There seemed to be no progress. Each move he made seemed to mean just more violence, more imprisonments. I had encountered him on a dark night of the soul. Next day he was confident and smiling again.

"You admire him?" she asked.

"Greatly. He's a good and courageous man. He knows that he's in danger every day, that someone might try to kill him any time—"

"Oh, no."

"They always kill the Goodies, never the Baddies. I'm sure President Kennedy will only go so far to help him."

"The President will go all the way."

"The Kennedys are white nouveau riche. They don't know much about black life."

"Don't be so prejudiced."

"It's the truth. Kennedy still talks about Negroes as *they.*"

"That's not true." She wouldn't hear a word against Kennedy. A young president with sex appeal was so rare, he

171

should be treasured, not criticized. "You're too conscious of it because of your black girl friend."

"I'm a little more objective than that." I spoke sharply because she'd irritated me. What she'd said was too easy. "Whites, particularly rich whites, know very little about how Negroes live. The Kennedys are no exception. Martin Luther King and others will have to educate them by risking their lives. But why should they? Why can't whites get out there and educate themselves?"

"The Kennedys know all about the situation already," she said.

"It isn't a *situation*," I said nastily. "It's human life— lives."

"You just wait and see. You're in for some surprises."

"I hope so." I sounded so solemn that I couldn't help grinning.

Either her spirits had risen or she was putting on a good show. I watched her without seeming to. She had fine eyes and such pretty eyebrows, and her nose always amused me. It conveyed her spunkiness. Surely, if she'd followed her nose, she'd never be prey to these depressions, those rushes of uncertainty about herself, about her future, about other people.

"Have you ever read Scott Fitzgerald's *Tender Is the Night?*" I asked her. Books seemed to be the safest topic.

"I don't think so. Why?"

"There's a great part for you in it. A film actress who—" I was on the point of saying "goes crazy" when I checked myself, remembering her mother and her own fears.

"Who what?"

"She marries and breaks down and then recovers and drops her husband. He's a doctor. The proof of her recovery is that she's strong enough to drop him." Then I remembered.

I had it wrong. The film actress didn't go crazy or marry the doctor. The actress and the wife were different women. Oh, what did it matter? But in my memory, the actress had a golden Monroe quality, although it had been a long time since I'd read the novel. It seemed to me that Fitzgerald had anticipated Monroe, or at least some aspects of her. Put the two female characters together and maybe you would get the whole of Monroe. She had already dropped her husband, but that wasn't a sign of recovery. She wasn't in good shape. She was going regularly to a psychiatrist, and the Strasbergs served much the same purpose. She would have given *Tender Is the Night* a different ending, but what?

"That's a nice title," she said. "The night *is* tender."

"The doctor drops from sight into the night of obscurity. The wife, for a time, escapes into a mental night—"

"That sounds familiar," she said jokingly. "There are times when I've fallen asleep at last and I hate to wake up and have to go through it all again. But that sounds gloomy."

It certainly didn't seem like a safe topic. I said quickly: "When I was a boy I wrote to Laurence Olivier, suggesting that the doctor would make a good role for him. He replied that he would look into it. I was crazy. The role needs an American."

"I wouldn't want to do it with Sir Olivier—or Lord Gielgud," she added with a grin.

"How about Montgomery Clift?"

"Two crazy people together."

"Have you any news of him?"

"Just the same old misfit. Monty the Misfit. Marilyn the Misfit." She giggled. "I don't think *The Misfits* is going to knock 'em over. First reactions are very mixed."

"Wait and see. It's too early."

"Famous last words." She looked serious. "Maybe I didn't have enough—you know—distance from the character. Arthur wrote me into it and our marriage was breaking up during that period. Maybe I was playing *me* too much, some ideal me—"

"But that's the Method, isn't it? Finding in yourself—"

"Finding experiences to help. But it can't be *you.* Maybe I was really playing me, and Arthur was writing how he saw me instead of a character—or how he saw me before we broke up. Roslyn now might be more of a bitch." She gave a sneaky, mischievous grin.

"It's still a pretty good movie."

"But a success is important. It gives you power."

"Still scared to be a loser, huh?"

She smiled. "Quoting my own words against me!" She sat back. "You know, you have a calming effect on me."

"I hope it's not just the interviewer's technique for getting people to talk. Interviewers pretend to be wide-eyed or innocent or smart or friendly, to relax the other person. But I'm not playing that game with you."

She patted my hand sympathetically. "I know you're not. You're quiet. You're a good listener. You don't want anything from me, which is rare. I feel relaxed with you. Sometimes I think the only people who stay with me and really listen are people I hire, people I pay. And that makes me sad. Why can't I have friends around me all the time, friends who want nothing from me?"

"You must have plenty of friends."

"Nobody has plenty of friends, not real friends. But friends have their own lives. Sometimes I want to talk to someone late at night and I call a friend and wake them up. They're very nice about it, but you know you're spoiling their rest, and when I say what about coming over or meeting some-

174

where, they tell me they have to get up early. I don't blame them. It's just that occasionally I feel like talking to someone when I can't sleep."

"You could always try me."

"At the Y? It took me long enough to get through to you during the day. I can guess what it would be like at three o'clock in the morning. And I'd wake you up, too! What I need is another husband. A man who's *there* all the time. But I'm not going to hurry into that again. It's often just enough to *be* with someone. I don't even need to touch them. Not even talk. A feeling passes between you both. You're not alone."

"There's an Indian saying: 'Silence also is conversation.' "

"But we Americans hate silence. We've got to have constant background noise. We're afraid of silence, afraid of being alone. I know I am. That's why silence is hard to achieve in the movies. People want what they want in life—action, noise."

"They always seem to like what you give them."

"Would they like it if I gave them Shakespeare? Do you think I could play Shakespeare? Tell me. Be truthful now."

"Sure you could."

My voice must have had a note of uncertainty, because she said: "Do you *really*, honestly, think so?"

She seemed anxious for confirmation, for support. I decided to be completely honest with her. I couldn't patronize her. I liked her too well.

"There's no question that you have the talent—and the ambition." Oh, what was I doing telling Marilyn Monroe she had talent! But it was too late to shut up. "Moviemaking requires one kind of stamina, and Shakespeare on stage another. The plays are so long, night after night. . . ." I let my voice trail away. She knew what I was saying.

"Maybe it's a matter of practice, of getting used to it. I had to get used to movies and"—laughing nervously—"I haven't done too bad. Could I remember all those lines? The poetry has a rhythm, and that helps."

"Why do you want to play Shakespeare? Is he worth all the trouble?"

She smiled uncertainly. "He's the greatest, isn't he? All actors and actresses want to play Shakespeare."

"I've always held it against Shakespeare that his rich people speak poetry and his poor people speak prose."

"You mean Shakespeare was an English snob?" Her eyes were as wide as if I had whistled in church.

"I don't know that I'd go that far. But if I had to be judged by a writer, I think I'd prefer Balzac."

She seized on that as a game she could find some release in. "I don't think I've ever met a writer I'd like as my judge. They observe people, but often they don't feel them. Arthur doesn't like people that much. But I think you've got to love people, all kinds of people, to be able to have an opinion about them that's worth anything. The whole idea of judging people is crazy. We do what we have to do, and we pay for it. We're no better than we have to be. We can *try* to be better, and part of trying is not to condemn other people."

"My mother won't kill anything. Not even a cockroach."

"I'm with your mother. I like that. Why shouldn't the roaches live?"

"That's probably because you haven't got any in your swell apartment."

"I've lived with lots of roaches," she said indignantly.

Her indignation made me laugh. "I bet you have."

"I certainly have. Big Hollywood roaches."

176

"Maybe you ought to play Archy and Mehitabel instead of Lady MacBeth."

"Archy and who?"

"It was a famous series about a literary cockroach."

"I'll stay with Lady MacBeth. It's one of the great roles for women, isn't it?"

"With Brando as MacBeth?"

"Maybe. Marlon's kinda hard to tie down, they say. He's never sure what he wants to do. He and Monty Clift have a lot in common, though they're totally different people, but they don't plan their careers too well and they're not ambitious enough for their talents. Both of them should be studying with Lee," she added primly.

"They seem afraid of the stage now. And maybe too temperamental—too much the star to take Strasberg's analyses in front of the other students."

"Oh, I think you're wrong. If I can do it, why can't they? I mean, to a lot of people I'm as big a star as they are, but"
—her eyes grew troubled—"I guess people don't take me as seriously."

"A lot of people never take a beautiful woman seriously."

"They think beauty is meant to serve them. I wrote a poem about that once. How people like to corrupt beauty, bring it down to their level. They don't know how rare it can be. Everyone can be beautiful in their own way, but most people don't let themselves be beautiful. Most people don't like themselves. . . ."

My notes for that meeting run out here. I don't remember how we left, except that no one recognized her. She wanted to meet again, and that surprised me. Surely she had close friends to unburden herself with. Perhaps being detached from her life helped—as if I were a surrogate psychiatrist. Her regular psychiatrist was in California, I think. I didn't know if she had a stand-in in New York. Perhaps not.

My money was fast running out, and it was nearly time to go. One of my big regrets about leaving New York was that my next meeting with Marilyn would have to be my last.

20

Walking along Eighth Avenue to the next meeting, I watched a cop harass a teenaged hippie with long, Jesus hair and a flower in his hat. The flower children, as they were getting to be known, really brought out all the hostility of a certain kind of older man hung up on his masculinity. It was as if the long hair and the flowers were a direct challenge to the way he lived and saw himself.

I mentioned it to Marilyn when she at last arrived, and she was instantly indignant. "Those big tough guys are so sick. They aren't even all that tough! They're afraid of kindness and gentleness and beauty. They always want to kill something to prove themselves! But the kids are changing. They're not swallowing it all any more. They're getting into other things."

"J.D. Salinger caught them well. Have you read any of his stories?"

She didn't reply. I didn't know whether it meant she knew Salinger's work or not. She always seemed to take it hard if you mentioned a book she hadn't read, as if it were proof of her ignorance. I hurried on.

"This cop was being so vicious that I tried to interrupt by asking what the kid had done. He pushed me away and said he'd take me in, too, if I said anything more. Put a uniform on some people and they think they've got a blank check to do anything."

"Oh, I wish I'd been there!" She was pink with annoyance. "Together, we could have beat him down." She clutched my hand impulsively and smiled.

"*Marilyn Monroe taken to jail,*" I said. "How would you like that headline, that kind of publicity?"

"I wouldn't mind if it was for a good cause."

I believed her.

She had invited me to have a farewell dinner before I left, but I told her I preferred another bar meeting. I imagined a dinner would include some of her friends at her apartment or be in a fancy restaurant where she would be recognized and fussed over, and I felt she was better in talk with just one other person. *I* certainly was, though that was probably the interviewer in me.

This last time, she had no makeup on, as usual, and her hair needed washing. There was also a faint body odor which I found exciting, but which many people wouldn't have. They would have regarded it as a sign of not taking proper care of herself, of not caring. Maybe she *didn't* care, if she was sleeping so badly and was on pills. Perhaps she was paying me the compliment of showing herself without any glossy aids.

"You know," she said, still upset about the cop, "I don't like Hemingway for that reason." She said it shyly, as though she didn't want me to think she was showing off her knowledge or was paying me back for mentioning Salinger. "People tell me he loves *shooting* animals and *killing* fish. I think a writer —an artist—should set an example. He shouldn't add to all the killing in the world. He should add to the love. That's what those kids are trying to do."

"Hemingway has a mystical approach to hunting—"

"The end is the same."

"In all his work he is obsessed with death."

"All the more reason not to add to it."

She was worked up, and if I went on obstinately defending him, I would soon be as culpable as Hemingway in her eyes. I beat a retreat. "Hemingway said once that if he hadn't done so much hunting, he might have killed himself."

"That might be better. It's a person's privilege. I don't believe it's a sin or a crime. It's your right if you want to, though it doesn't get you anywhere." She smiled. "Unless you believe in heaven and hell, but I sorta believe they're right here, right now. You possess yourself, but you never possess other people or animals. You've got no right to end *their* lives."

"Not even to eat?"

"We can all be vegetarians."

"Vegetables, plants, have life."

She looked hurt, as if I was merely being smart and missing her point, so I said quickly: "I guess you're right."

"How's your friend down south?" she asked.

"No real news. She writes that sometimes it's hard to see any progress."

"She's right. It's the same in your own life. Sometimes I think I was more in control of my life years and years ago, and yet one should make progress; one should learn more every year and become . . . well, if not happier, then calmer and more able to handle your problems. But I'm not. Sometimes I just seem to make more problems for myself." She looked mischievous. "I do. It makes me feel I haven't grown up as much as I should have by now."

"You're afraid of not feeling."

"How did you know?"

"It's the impression you give."

"I don't want to be bland and just shrug everything off the way so many people do, especially in Hollywood. You tell them something and they say, 'yeah, sure,' as if they knew it all along and you're a dope not to have known it. I like people who can be surprised and don't try to hide it and enjoy what's going on. But there are times when I want to be alone. I used to be afraid of being alone, but not now. I spend more and more time alone—trying to sleep." A laugh, but not a gay one. "I'm getting too serious. You'll be telling people Marilyn is too gloomy to drink with."

"Never. I don't talk about our talks. You lose things if you talk about them."

"Not always. Sometimes."

"Often."

"It seems to me I was much more open when I was younger. Now I don't trust people as much, even when I seem to."

"You've got to know who to trust."

"How do you do that? Have they got labels?"

"You can spot the phonies."

"Not always in show business. We're acting all the time."

"You talk as if you haven't grown."

"My body has, but sometimes I feel the inner me—and my mind—haven't."

"Just look at your films. Compare *The Misfits* to your early movies, like *Niagara* or *Don't Bother to Knock.*"

"That's acting—"

"Your talent is you."

"But I feel"—she groped for the words, as if it meant a lot to her—"me, myself, I'm not as mature as I should be. There's a part of me that has never developed and keeps on getting in the way, getting me in lousy situations, screwing up relationships, stopping my rest. I think about it all the time. My mother wasn't strong-minded. Maybe what I'm talking about is a weak-minded quality I inherited from her. Oh, I

184

don't know." She looked suddenly embarrassed. "Maybe I don't even know what I'm talking about. Don't let me spoil things."

"You're not spoiling anything. I enjoy talking seriously with you." She might just have been using me as a sounding board, but I felt flattered that she talked to me this way. That might be doing her an injustice, but I didn't want to exaggerate our relationship. I would miss our meetings more than she would. "Don't forget," I said, thinking back to what she had said, "lots of writers have warned us about these different parts of ourselves. Jekyll and Hyde. Dostoevski's the other—"

"You mean I'm really no different from anyone else," she said jokingly, touching my hand. "And there I was thinking I was special!"

"Nobody is." I grinned. I didn't want to seem to be trying to flatter her. She wasn't in the mood. Her face looked tired, yet she had a vitality that could transform her appearance in a moment. She hadn't wanted to meet that day. She had some kind of business meeting, and she was seeing Strasberg. But when she knew I was leaving, she squeezed me into her schedule and was only about an hour late. I remembered what Clark Gable had told me at the end of the filming of *The Misfits*, when her tardiness was only a memory. He said he didn't bear her any ill will for having kept him waiting: "She's worth waiting for." Probably he was telling me that to show that the King could be magnanimous, and perhaps he told his wife something else in the privacy of their home; but Gable was essentially a kind man, and what he said was true. I fumed over the lost hour, growing bored with the bar and the crawling finger of the clock, but when she arrived, out of breath and full of apologies, she transformed the whole scene. One seemed to acquire a little of her vitality and her urge to have a good time against all odds. I had seen her in many moods, including her bitchy one, but this quality stood out in the end. It was one reason why her death saddened me so much. Someone who had such a talent for enjoying herself—what John Huston (and my father) called "heart"—should not have been cut short in her life. She was late, but she always made up for it.

She asked me if I'd ever met Carl Sandburg.

No, but I mentioned Robert Frost. I told her how, when Frost had received an honorary degree from a leading university, he'd said: "I'd rather receive a degree from you fellers than an education."

She loved that. Her laughter rose so high that heads down the bar turned and looked at us.

Had I ever met Edith Sitwell?

No, none of the Sitwells.

"I expected her to be a real English snob, but she wasn't. She was what my mother would have called a Lady. A grand lady, strong enough to stand up to men. Negroes who are grown-up rightly resent being called *boy,* but think of all the women who are called *girl.* Some men call you a good girl in the same way they pet their dog." She laughed gaily and said that I was not to take that personally. "I remember one old Hollywood producer who petted me as if I *was* his pet dog. He was sort of sick. We were all warned about him. I guess long ago he wanted a bit of love and he never found it, but he was looking the wrong way by the time I met him. He'd never find it!"

"Are all the stories about the casting couch true?"

"They can be. You can't sleep your way into being a star, though. It takes much, much more. But it helps. A lot of actresses got their first chance that way. Most of the men are such horrors, they deserve all they can get out of them!" She

186

said this defiantly, as if I were thinking of a critical reply. How could I prove that I was really a nice, open guy?

She made me want to seem as nice a guy as possible to her. She always put me on my best behavior. I felt that if I were suddenly mean or intolerant, she would be shocked. Yet she could be that way herself. I asked her why she had bitched out someone I knew on the set of one of her earlier movies—a shy, well-meaning man who had taken it badly.

"I can be a monster," she replied seriously. Then she was funny at her own expense, contorting her face and grimacing as Marilyn the Monster. "You know how sometimes you try to be the person people want you to be?" she said. "Some of my friends want me to be innocent and shy, and I find that's the way I am with them. If they saw the monster in me, they'd probably never talk to me again. Sometimes I think that's what happened in my marriage to Arthur. When we were first married, he saw me as so beautiful and innocent among the Hollywood wolves that I tried to be like that. I almost became his student in life and literature, the way I'm Lee's student for acting. But when the monster showed, Arthur couldn't believe it. I disappointed him when that happened. But I felt he knew and loved all of me. I wasn't sweet all through. He should love the monster, too. But maybe I'm too demanding. Maybe there's no man who could put up with all of me. I put Arthur through a lot, I know. But he also put me through a lot. It's never one-sided. You can't have two people trying to make it together without that, without a lot of pain. It would have been easier for me with a more party-going kind of man, but that would only be easy for one side of me. I have had them, and next day it's all empty. It's party time or no time. I want more from a man, from another human being. I want someone who thinks, who's aware, who'll be interesting after twenty years.

187

Someone different from me. A challenge."

Then she must have feared that she was looking too much inward and excluding me, for she added, with a bright friendly look: "You seem to be the same with your friend in the South. That's a challenge for you. Some people choose a man or a woman like themselves and after a few months it's like a marriage of twins. I don't want that. But when I'm tired or upset, I run for cover and I find myself going out with party people who can laugh and joke and give you a good time for a short while and bring no worries. I know a lot of guys like that in Hollywood, but in the end it's so empty. *Empty!* I feel like I'm rejecting part of myself, that I'm letting part of me die, like a dead branch that gets no chance to grow and develop. Of course you can go too much the other way; I've done that, too. Spend all your time with the brains, playing their audience. Some of Arthur's friends accepted me immediately, but some of them treated me like a dull little sex object with no brains and talked to me like a high school principal with a backward student. Later for you. In my life it's been hard to find the in-between. Too often it's been either-or. You get driven to extremes and I don't want that. I want some calmness, some steadiness, in my life, and for a time I had that in my life with Arthur. That was a nice time. And then we lost it."

Marilyn stopped abruptly, quiet, thinking. She made thinking seem like a serious, deliberate process, the kind of attitude people usually have toward doing push-ups or taking the dog for a walk. When I say that, some people who never got over seeing her as a dumb blonde will assume that I'm implying she found thinking difficult. Quite the opposite. She gave thinking her serious attention. I wanted to interrupt her in case her thoughts were regretful or melancholy, but I didn't wish to cut in too abruptly. I watched her carefully. Her tongue

188

played along her bottom lip. Her thoughts were far from the bar. Who could have guessed at that moment that she was a movie star? She looked like a housewife with problems.

"Marilyn," I said.

The use of her name—I had so seldom used it, being slow to use first names—brought her back to the bar. She grinned ruefully, as if she had been caught daydreaming in class.

"I'm taking a lot of sleeping pills these days and they make me feel dopey sometimes. But I'm back with you again," and she flashed me a smile that lifted both her and my spirits up a notch. "It can become a habit, but if you can't sleep, what are you supposed to do? You feel so lifeless next morning. Nobody's really ever been able to tell me why I sleep so badly, but I know once I begin thinking, it's goodbye, sleep. I used to think exercise helped—being in the country, fresh air, being with a man, sharing—but sometimes I can't sleep *whatever* I'm doing, unless I take some pills. And then it's only a drugged sleep. It's not the same as really sleeping."

This seemed a bad subject to get on, so I interrupted it with an offhand question: "What are you studying now?"

"You mean with Lee?"

"Yes, or what are you reading?" Sometimes simple questions seemed to get complicated with her.

"I've been reading the sonnets of Shakespeare. Some are beautiful and some seem kinda ordinary. But then you don't like Shakespeare anyway," she teased.

"I didn't say I didn't like him. I don't like what we've done with him." I decided to ask her a question I'd often wanted to: "Do you find Michael Chekhov and Lee Strasberg very different as teachers?"

She thought about it. "I think they have the same aims," she said at last; "but one is an actor and the other a director.

189

Therefore their approach is a little different." She smiled. "I speak as if Mr. Chekhov is still alive. Well, he is—to me."

I wondered if it was a diplomatic answer, but maybe there was no conflict of loyalties.

"Didn't Lee Strasberg do some acting in the Group Theater days? And Michael Chekhov must have directed productions?"

"Oh, yes, but I meant where their greatest interest lay. Mr. Chekhov was such a great actor. . . ." She reflected a moment and sighed. "His name should be world famous. There should be statues of him. Yet hardly anyone knows about him." Her expression reminded me of the way she had looked when someone was trying to kill a moth in the bar in Reno the first time I met her. The ways of the world could be hard to take. "He gave me some confidence in myself. I had none at all. People didn't take me seriously—or they only took my body seriously. But, Mr. Chekhov showed me that I really had talent and that I needed to develop it. You didn't know how much you had, or in what direction, until you worked at it. I thought of paying for a statue of him myself, to put up in New York, but it wouldn't be taken seriously, just coming from one person."

"Only the pigeons like statues."

"Then have a drama school named after him. It's shameful to treat his memory that way!" I was beginning to regret getting her on the subject of Chekhov. "Can't you do something in your newspaper?" she asked.

"Not unless something happens. Newspapers don't as a rule make events. They just report them. Also, they're mainly interested in people who are still alive."

"Michael Chekhov is still alive! He's immortal!"

"At least Lee Strasberg has his own studio."

But she wouldn't be diverted so easily. "Maybe I should get a petition signed by everybody in show business. Get all my friends to sign it and then send it to the President. I'm sure President Kennedy would want to do something for Mr. Chekhov."

"He might if you asked him personally."

"You think so?" She looked serious. I could imagine her, petition in hand, knocking at the White House door. She was persistent when she wanted to be, too persistent if you weren't as interested as she was. I could imagine that it might get on a husband's nerves. The difference between her teachers that I had had in mind was that Chekhov, I had been told, thought of her as a movie actress who needed better, deeper roles but did not see her as a great stage actress, as Strasberg did. I mentioned this to her, partly to get off the subject of Kennedy. She reminded me of a star-struck girl at the mention of the President's name. I thought again of the super-sophisticated Simone Signoret; she wouldn't have been so openly impressed by anyone, least of all a politician.

"Mr. Chekhov didn't talk much about the stage," she said carefully, "but I was younger then. Several of the roles we studied and played were for the theater. He had no wish to limit me," she added, giving me a disapproving look.

"I didn't mean to suggest that he didn't think—" Oh, I was getting tied up in negatives.

"But you're quite right," she said generously, trying to help me out. "Mr. Chekhov thought much more of the movies than Lee does. Lee distrusts the movies, at least in my case."

"But you've mastered movie technique."

"What good is that if you're not free to make the movies you want to?"

"And you think you'll be freer in the theater?"

"I hope so."

A brief silence. She wasn't brooding now. I sensed that she wanted to leave.

"Should we get some air?" I said.

"Oh, yes!" she cried, as if I had suggested something wonderful that had never occurred to her.

We quickly left the bar. A man followed us out, a middle-aged man, in what looked like a mailman's uniform minus the cap.

"Pardon me," he said politely, "but are you Marilyn Monroe?"

In her position I would have been tempted to deny it, but she gave him a pleased smile, not at all brassy or automatic, and we didn't get away until she had given him her autograph on the back of an envelope. He went back in the bar to tell everybody, and we walked quickly up the block. The encounter seemed to have done her good. She beamed and looked much more like Marilyn Monroe. We didn't get far. She couldn't pass an old wino with brown skin and grey whiskers. She thrust a dollar in his hand and engaged him in conversation. She wanted to know where he was staying—in the park—and what his favorite drink was—Wild Irish Rose—and whether he had a cure for insomnia (Wild Irish Rose). Most of her questions seemed to be asked on impulse. They might have been conversing at ease in her apartment. I soon felt excluded by their brisk chatter.

"Marilyn," I interrupted, seeing some of the men come out of the bar, "should I get you a cab?"

"Okay," she said. "Please excuse me," she told the wino; "I'm terribly late."

"Will you tell me your name?" the battered old man asked her.

"Marilyn," she said simply.

I was sure he would recognize her then and draw a crowd, but all he said was, "A pretty name for a pretty woman."

"What is your name?" she asked.

"James Brown," he said, pleased.

"A famous name," she said.

I had a cab for her by then. She kissed me lightly on the lips, said, "Bon voyage, call me when you get back," and was gone.

Side by side, the wino and I watched her cab disappear. "A doll," he said.

I went away to Europe and from that distance, glimpsed through friends' letters or the movie gossip columns, she seemed more than ever to be poised at a crossroads, not knowing which way to take. I heard that she had spent a couple of weeks in a hospital for rest and to get off pills. It sounded like the kind of breakdown she had had on *The Misfits*. But friends of hers insisted that she was now "fine" and "keen to get back to work." I wondered to what extent she was playing a role, giving them what they wanted to see. She was good at that. But surely another breakdown and hospitalization would awaken again all her dreams about ending up like her mother in a mental hospital. How much could she take and still function in the highly competitive film world where someone was always waiting to take your place? My old feeling of admiration had changed to one of sympathy—or was it pity, a feeling I didn't like to have for anyone?

I waited for an announcement of some ambitious stage production, masterminded by Lee Strasberg. My nightmare scenario had her withdrawing from rehearsals or breaking down on opening night. I could see her standing above the footlights, the loneliest figure in the world, mouth open but wordless, her memory groping as a hidden prompter tried to feed her her lines.

But no announcements were made and there was no news from Hollywood. *The Misfits* was in the moviehouses and not doing very well. The reviews had been mixed; her dramatic performance had not won her the recognition she had hoped for. I went to see the movie but couldn't be critical. In some ways it was like seeing a home movie. I was too close to it. Too many scenes brought back too many memories, particularly the exchanges between Marilyn and Montgomery Clift. I was too sympathetic to both of them—both sensitive people who would forever find it hard to cope with the world.

Her divorce was now final, and Arthur Miller had married again—a photographer, Inga Morath, who had covered part of the making of *The Misfits* for Magnum, a photo agency. I met them briefly together. Miller looked much older but less strained. His new wife couldn't have been less like Marilyn; he might almost have deliberately selected her opposite. She was European—dark, slim, intellectual. She appeared efficient and independent, sophisticated and fashionably cynical. In the glimpses I had of their relationship, Miller was definitely the head of the household, a nice change after his long, grim months of tending to Marilyn.

I didn't mention her and neither did they. I wondered whether Miller had changed or whether I had. Perhaps he was a man who was very much influenced by the kind of woman he was married to, and this new wife was certainly different. She pressed me in a friendly way to stay longer or return soon, but Miller said nothing. He was impassive, detached, remote. Perhaps now I was merely a reminder of troubled days that he'd like to forget.

I asked him if he had any more movie plans, and he shook his head with a grim expression. Almost all his writing life had been devoted to the theater, as Marilyn's life had been devoted to the movies. His unhappy experience in Hollywood might have seemed a warning to her now of what to expect if she turned to the theater. But I thought she wouldn't heed warnings. She'd follow her instinct. It had made her a star, hadn't it? That was what she might think. But she was no longer the woman she had been. In the old days she would have made another movie by now; *The Misfits* would merely be her last movie but one. Now, though, it was as if she had gone into semiretirement. People were wondering if she would make a "comeback."

The TV production of *Rain*, to be directed by Lee Strasberg, was canceled. Eventually plans were announced for a Hollywood movie, fittingly entitled *Something's Got to Give*. Marilyn began it and then got fired for "willful violation of contract." She was late, she was sick, and she took time off to sing at President Kennedy's birthday party at Madison Square Garden (where Peter Lawford introduced her as "the late Marilyn Monroe"—a simple in-joke then, but later a grim prophecy). It was *The Misfits* behavior all over again, but this time she wasn't working for her own group and studio executives weren't as sympathetic.

I also picked up rumors of some personal involvement with her adored Kennedys—some said with the President, some thought with Robert Kennedy, some said with both of them. I hoped none of it was true. The Kennedys were tough and ambitious, Catholic and married. She could only get hurt; no affair could have a future. She needed a relationship she could hold onto for a long time.

But long before rumors and truth began to sort themselves out (or as much as they ever would among people who had so much to lose), I made a quick visit to New York at a time when she was there, too.

I was prepared for a polite brush-off if I tried to get in touch with her. Her life had probably changed as much as Miller's. The cynic in me said she had only been using me

199

when she needed someone to talk to. Now she probably had someone else, perhaps another journalist sworn to secrecy. But I was mistaken. She was immediately friendly, and suggested meeting as soon as possible. "I want to catch up with all that's happened to you," she said. I suggested the bar at the Algonquin, but she insisted on the old bar on Eighth Avenue. "Never drop a good thing," she said. Her voice sounded tired.

An earlier meeting with a friend at the United Nations began late and went on for longer than intended, so I was about fifteen minutes overdue when I succeeded in getting a cab and began the crosstown traffic crawl. I wasn't worried about being late. Fifteen minutes late was as good as being early, by Marilyn Monroe's standards. But when I walked into the bar, she was already there, sitting in our old booth at the rear. I was astonished. It was worth a headline: MARILYN EARLY! I remembered that other headline that had annoyed me so much: MARILYN'S HUSBAND IN GALWAY. That seemed a lifetime ago.

I could see the change in her as I walked toward her. Her body had lost some of the shape and sap of youth. Her face lacked some of its former fullness. The skin seemed more stretched over the bones, less shiny with health. There was a delicate, worn air about her now. She had some makeup on this time, but it didn't hide the tiredness or the lines, and she must have known it. I've read accounts by people who saw her during the last weeks before her death, and they insist she was in good spirits and looked well. But I couldn't believe that the woman I saw had changed so much. Some of the last photographs show that her body had begun a permanent drift into middle age, even though she okayed only those in which she thought she looked good. One photographer, saying that Marilyn's body had become "mature," added that Marilyn seemed tragically blind to the fact. Perhaps in the Narcissus mood she needed for those photographic sessions, she couldn't sap her self-confidence by admitting anything; but I'm sure she was aware of the change. My last conversation with her suggested as much. Middle age was beckoning at a time when she wasn't strong, and too many personal involvements of a dangerous nature were threatening to weaken her even more.

Had her fear that her beauty wouldn't last much longer driven her into these involvements? Was her feeling that of someone having a last fling? I know what the answer would be from those old friends who insisted at the end that she was well and full of plans, denying the suggestion of suicide (as they would later deny the allegations of murder), but I have only the evidence of this last meeting.

She kissed me lightly and gaily. I bought us drinks. She said "good luck" and we touched glasses. She remembered Christine and asked about her. I said Christine's letters were increasingly depressed; her friends were being beaten up and jailed for demonstrating.

"It seems unbelievable unless you've witnessed it," she said. "Some things you've just gotta see. Why don't you go down to see her again?"

I said I couldn't get time off from the paper and that I was hoping for some big event in the South to take me down there.

"If it's the money," she said, "I could lend you some. Pay back when you make your first million."

"That's a nice offer."

"I'm serious."

"I know you are, and I'm very grateful."

"Don't be grateful. Do it."

I shook my head, smiling. "I just don't like borrowing."

"You need to see her," she persisted. "No friendship can

live by letters alone. That was why so many marriages went bust in the war."

"I'll see her soon."

"You men are so heartless."

She was putting on a show of being light-hearted, of being happy; but I had an impression of someone very fragile being held together by willpower.

"Did you know Arthur's married again?" she asked.

I said I had met them.

"How did you like his wife?"

I was as careful as I would have been walking through a mine field. "She was friendly."

"A little bit remains even when you break up," she said. "You can't let go completely. It takes time, I guess. You feel that he's wiping out the past with you by marrying again, and that's silly. We live in the present; we can't go on living in the past. Arthur and I could never live together again. It's over. Why shouldn't he get married again? Maybe I'll get married again myself," she said with a mysterious smile. She seemed secretly serious, looking at me to see how I reacted.

"Have you someone in mind? Is there a leading candidate?"

"Sort of." She played with her drink and I thought: she is still beautiful. Her expression was so wistful as she looked down, dreaming. Then she glanced up and laughed. "Only problem is, he's married right now. And he's famous; so we have to meet in secret." Her tone of voice suggested that she found that exciting, romantic.

"And he's getting a divorce?"

"Arthur had to get a divorce, you know." That didn't answer my question, but I let it go. It wasn't an interview; I didn't have to pursue any news. But I was concerned about her mention of someone famous and married. Were the Kennedy stories true, then? Poor Marilyn, if they were. I didn't know how to reply. Every professional instinct threw up leading questions, but personally I preferred not to know. It wasn't my business. I didn't want to bother her. Let her tell me what she wanted to. Something in her wanted to boast about it, or worry over it, even though it was a secret. But how could you keep a secret in gossipy Hollywood?

"He's in politics," she said, going as near the point of telling me his name as she could.

"In Hollywood?"

"Oh, no." She giggled at my ignorance. "In Washington."

Okay, so it sounded like one of the Kennedys. JFK had a reputation as a woman-chaser, but I'd never heard it of the much more uptight Bobby. If either of them was involved with her, it could only be a passing affair, an irresistible scalp for a womanizer or a vacation from the wife and kids for the younger brother. For her, it was bound to be so much more serious. Her pride wouldn't allow her to seem of only passing interest. Yet people behave strangely when they come close to great power, and Marilyn had a lively imagination. Was she giving herself the role of a Madame de Pompadour? A king's mistress? Did she go beyond that and imagine herself as the First Lady? Surely she could find security in the White House. It might even set her inferiority complex finally to rest. But she also had a sharp sense of proportion, a reliable sense of humor, which, even close to great power, would keep her thinking realistically. She didn't know politicians, however, the way she knew Hollywood executives. Could she fool herself so much that she would head for a worse betrayal from a man than any she had seen so far? She always tended to see her failed relationships as betrayals. I hoped I had it wrong. Maybe it was a passing affair with a senator or an ambassador, and all would be well. Maybe a happy marriage would even come out of it. But I didn't really believe that. The gossip was too persistent not to have some truth in it. Poor Marilyn. That day I wanted to reach out and help, to say: "Stop. Turn back." But there was nothing I could do except listen.

"Are you planning anything for Broadway?" I asked, trying for a safer topic. "I heard you worked on a Colette scene at the studio. What a woman she was!"

She wasn't interested in Colette at that moment, though the French writer seemed like the kind of woman who would have appealed to Marilyn. "I'm thinking about movies now," she said.

"Your plans have changed?"

"The theater reaches so few people. A few hundred a night, that's all. You have to play for months and years to reach the people a movie can reach in one night."

I was impatient with this numbers game, which seemed so unlike her, and I showed it. "That sounds more like politics than art. You're not trying to win votes, are you? In the arts you have to pay for your freedom—"

But she wasn't listening. "My friend says I have immense power and I should use it. I have an audience of millions all over the world. I can reach all the people. But I can only do it through movies. He says I should stick to movies. I think he's right." She patted her head scarf. "I wasn't well for awhile, and it made me think. I can make a movie in a few weeks and it's all over. In the theater I'd have to go on for years, night after night, well or sick. It's not the best use of my time. . . ."

I had thought that myself, but I didn't like to hear it from her. It was as if she were limiting her aspirations, as if the ambitious careerist side of her were trying to suppress the other side. Was it all the influence of this new man in her life or had she decided to give up some of her dreams because they weren't possible? I couldn't answer that and I couldn't ask her. I just wished her well, wished it would turn out all right. But was this the attitude for her to take into middle age? Her "power" would go with her looks. What would be left? Her scenario for old age had included character acting and the theater. But facing age with this attitude, she might lose every-thing—like a defeated president who is no longer loved by enough voters to have the White House and can't be satisfied any longer with anything less.

I tried again to change the subject. Because we had once talked about Hemingway, I mentioned his suicide. Too late, I realized that this wasn't a good subject either. She wasn't sympathetic: "You shoot animals and then you shoot yourself."

"His father shot himself, too."

"He was probably a hunter, too. Did Hemingway have any children?"

"Three sons."

"They're probably worried that it runs in the family. I know how that is, from my mother's mental trouble. I worried for years that I would become like her. But everybody is differ-ent. Nothing is ever repeated the same way. If Hemingway's sons are hunters, too, someone should tell them to give it up and they'll be all right. The animals always get their revenge."

Her lack of sympathy for Hemingway irritated me, and I tried to tease her, though I should have known better. A dogmatic tone, so unlike her, should have warned me.

"How do you think President Kennedy is doing?" I asked.

"Wonderfully."

"He's made some bad appointments in the South. Christine's mad."

"I'm sure President Kennedy had good reasons."

"Yeah, he was paying off some political debts."

"You don't like President Kennedy?"

"It's not a matter of like or dislike with a president. It's whether he does a good job for *all* the people. It's too early to tell with Kennedy."

"I think he's going to be another Lincoln."

Her enthusiasm depressed me. It was the Arthur Miller story all over again. She built people up too high and in time was bound to be disappointed. Why couldn't she learn from someone like Simone Signoret? Yet it was precisely this innocence that got her into trouble, that made her more lovable, certainly much more so than any other celebrity I'd met.

"Do you feel like walking?" I asked her, dejected and therefore restless.

"Not in the streets."

"How about Central Park?"

"Okay."

I had to make a quick visit to the men's room. When I returned, a burly man I had noticed staring at us from the bar was leaning over the table, talking to her. Thinking she was a prostitute off Eighth Avenue, he was making a clumsy, drunken pass at her. I was angry (she didn't look like that!), and I shouted at him. He could have taken me apart with one hand, but he must have been embarrassed by his mistake, because he went meekly back to the bar.

She wasn't worried; she seemed rather pleased. "Well, you're not scared of being a loser, anyway," she said with a grin. It was nice to see her amused. We left the bar in high spirits.

We took a cab up Eighth Avenue to Central Park. The driver was a young guy with a beard. I saw him watching her in his mirror. I wondered if we would make the park before recognition dawned. We didn't. When I stopped him at 59th Street, he stared back at her and asked the inevitable question.

Pleased, she smiled and nodded. This was better than being taken for an Eighth Avenue whore. He wanted an autograph, which he got. He was shy with her but familiar, too, as if he had a personal connection. A lot of her fans seemed to feel that way. Marilyn was one of them.

The encounter with someone admiring made her feel good. She walked into the park with her head high, smiling.

"Is that the power you talked about?" I said with a grin. "One vote for Marilyn?"

"It makes me feel I must be doing something right," she said.

We sat on a bench and watched some pigeons and a solitary sparrow searching for food.

"I wish we had something for them," she said.

A man nearby was selling bags of potato chips so I bought a bag and gave it to her. She threw a handful at the birds. The pigeons were faster and bigger and the sparrow was shut out. Marilyn tossed a special big piece over to the sparrow, which pecked at it and tried to fly away with it, but it was too heavy. When he dropped it, a pigeon seized it.

"I've always identified with sparrows," she said, throwing the sparrow another, smaller piece.

The bag was soon empty.

"Let's go and find the squirrels," she said. We didn't have to walk far under the trees. A squirrel ran down a tree trunk to investigate. "How are you, bright eyes?" The squirrel obviously didn't want compliments, but food, so we had to walk back and buy another bag of potato chips. Soon she had several squirrels at her feet. They didn't think too highly of the potato chips, but beggars couldn't be choosers.

"If we were Hemingway, maybe we'd shoot them," she said.

"If we were President Kennedy," I replied, "we'd shake their hands and kiss their babies."

She didn't laugh. "You really don't like him," she said, as though she couldn't believe it.

"You don't like Hemingway."

"That's different."

"Why is it different?"

"Did you ever meet Hemingway?"

"No, but when I was a boy, he once wrote me a letter."

"What about?"

"I had read *The Sun Also Rises,* in which he says a bull was attracted by the color of the bullfighter's cape."

"A red rag to a bull."

"But my father told me bulls were color blind, so I wrote to ask Hemingway who was right. He sent back a long letter in which he didn't answer the question, really, but discussed his experiences with bulls and eagles. Bulls, he said, had no depth of vision. They saw only in two-dimensional silhouettes. Then he ended by wishing my father good luck."

"That was nice of him to go to such trouble for a boy. He must have been a nicer man than he seems."

"Maybe you've been misled by his image, as people are by yours."

She grinned. "Maybe you've been misled by President Kennedy's image."

"As an old reporter, I can't hero-worship either politicians or cops. I've seen too much of them."

"Have you ever met President Kennedy?"

"I've seen him in action."

"That's not the same as meeting him—as knowing him."

"You know him?"

She didn't reply but instead concentrated on the squirrels. I wished she had only squirrels in her life. She seemed so calm and untroubled at that moment. But squirrels were a lot of smart, pushy hustlers: they'd probably betray her in the end, too. She certainly brought out one's protective instinct. To survive, most people have to strike a balance between accepting the world for what it is and their hopes for an improvement; but Marilyn never seemed to achieve that balance. She went to extremes, either seeing the world as hopeless or building up hopes that couldn't possibly be fulfilled. Career woman one moment, disillusioned idealist the next. Yet she was always searching, and she looked everywhere: in the face of a wino or the President or a squirrel in the park. Nothing living was alien to her. I hoped she never gave up feeling that way and let the drugs take over. I examined her clear, blue eyes as she watched the squirrels. If she was back on heavy doses of sleeping pills, she didn't show it. She was out to look her best for the new man in her life and he, I thought, was the trouble she was unprepared for.

She decided it was time to go. I walked her back to 59th Street. I offered to walk her home, but she preferred to take a cab. The crosstown streets were busy and, walking, she would probably have been recognized countless times.

She kissed me and wished me luck and told me to call her if I came to Los Angeles.

She wasn't coming back to New York?

Not for a long time.

What about the Actors Studio?

She shrugged.

"Wish *me* luck," she said.

I wished her all the luck in the world.

She smiled at me through the cab window. She looked better for the walk in the park.

I waved until the cab was gone. I knew where the cab was taking her, but I wondered where her life was going. She was putting on a brave show, but what was behind it? Had she really reached a dead end?

The rumors kept circulating through the early part of 1962. She was supposed to be meeting Bobby Kennedy at Peter Lawford's place. Lawford, a longtime Hollywood actor, was married to one of Kennedy's sisters at that time. I once watched him make a film with Charles Laughton. During every break in the shooting, he had a small radio pressed against his ear, listening to a speech Kennedy was making somewhere—at the United Nations, I think. I couldn't believe he was so fascinated by the political clichés and assumed that he was just giving a good performance as Kennedy's brother-in-law for the rest of us. If the rumors were true and he had encouraged an affair between Marilyn and Bobby Kennedy, I was against him and so I enjoyed remembering how Marilyn's old hero, Charles Laughton, had upstaged him. During some of Lawford's lines, Laughton scratched his ear, a bit of business designed to steal the eventual movie audience's attention away from Lawford. The director, Otto Preminger, patiently pointed this out to Mr. Laughton. So in the next take, he left his ear alone—and ruffled his hair.

Then the rumors had Kennedy going cold on Marilyn—the obvious next step. Stories had her calling him at the Justice Department in Washington (he was still attorney general) and getting no call back. Another story had him describing her to someone as "a dumb broad." I was never a great admirer of Bobby Kennedy's sensitive perceptions—in my experience of him in those days, he seemed to be a tough rich boy, Boston

Irish, end-justifies-the-means politician—and so I was willing to believe he might say something as absurdly male chauvinist as that. I could imagine how Marilyn's giant inferiority complex would take such a rejection from one of her beloved Kennedys. Her longtime friend, Robert F. Slatzer, whom she once planned to marry, says in his book, *The Life and Curious Death of Marilyn Monroe*, that she told him Robert Kennedy had promised to marry her. Could she possibly believe that Kennedy would ruin himself politically for her?

I had wondered in the park that day where her life was going. It was only a few months later that we all knew. A newspaper editor telephoned me the news: she had been found lying dead across her bed in the small house she had bought in Los Angeles. It wasn't known whether she had committed suicide or died from an accidental overdose. Either was possible.

I didn't have time to do any remembering. The newspaper wanted a long obituary and would phone back for me to dictate it in half an hour. I sat at a typewriter, and for a few minutes my mind refused to function. Luckily, the newspaper's impersonal style meant that I didn't have to deal with my own feelings.

Marilyn Monroe's death at thirty-six is a real Hollywood tragedy, unlike most of those the film studios try to fabricate. It seems now to have the same inevitability as Hemingway's a year earlier, and just as death by shotgun gave his life a classical finish, so an overdose of sleeping pills seems now the only ending we might have expected to this tragedy. The heartrending fact is that many of the friends of this doomed film actress have been afraid for over a year that something like this might happen, and nobody seemed able to help. At least the gossip columnists who had begun to ask "What will Marilyn do when she's middle-aged?" have their answer now. . . .

I hadn't finished when the phone rang, so I had to make up the ending as I was dictating, which is hard on your prose. The best I could manage was: " 'Heart' is the word that comes to mind in trying to describe her as a person—she perhaps responded and felt too much for her own good. . . ." I put in something about her marriages ("Not for her those inbred Hollywood marriages") and added that after breaking up with Arthur Miller, Norma Jeane Mortensen seemed "alone in the crowd—the crowd of Hollywood symbols (and symbols of our society?) bearing down on her."

None of the words seemed to get close to her. It was one of those journalistic situations in which you knew what you should have said when you'd passed the deadline. I wished I could have given everyone a picture of her smiling through the cab window that last time I saw her.

I mentioned Dame Sybil Thorndike's admiration for her as a film actress and this led to a correspondence with that great old veteran of the theater (she had been Bernard Shaw's original St. Joan). Dame Sybil, who acted with Marilyn in *The Prince and the Showgirl* (during which Marilyn had her falling out with Olivier), said: "You watch her do it in the studio and it doesn't seem much—too vague and underplayed. But when you see it on the screen, her performance seems perfect. She really opens out. It's as if she were made for the cinema." But not for the theater?

Later that day I had to give a radio tribute, and Sean O'Casey, who was nearly blind and listened to the radio a great deal, heard it and pleased me by saying it conveyed the emotion he felt himself. The old Irish dramatist later said to me: "Who killed Marilyn Monroe—that's a question. That was a tragedy that affected me very much. I hate the idea of Hollywood in which she had to survive. She said she wanted to meet me when she was over here, and I wish I had. I would have liked to have talked with her."

"Perhaps you could have helped her, dear," said Mrs. O'Casey.

"Sometimes one can help another person," he responded. "Who knows? It's so easy to be foolish and so hard to be wise. I never knew she had such a hard upbringing—all those foster homes, never a real one."

"It was incredible that it didn't make her hard and bitter," I said.

"Oh," said O'Casey, "bitterness is no good to you. You only lose if you're bitter."

Who killed Marilyn Monroe? It was the first time I had heard the question put so bluntly. The controversy immediately after her death was about whether it had been suicide or an accident. Arthur Miller, like most of her friends, seemed to think it was an accidental overdose. I wrote briefly to him and he replied briefly. There was nothing to say that wasn't obvious.

Miller didn't go to the funeral. It was a strange affair— very small, very exclusive, arranged by former husband, Joe DiMaggio, the old baseball star, who had become friends with her again during the last year or two. DiMaggio was said to have been very much against her Kennedy involvement and her Hollywood friends who encouraged it. He excluded them all from the funeral. The only trouble was, it seemed far too exclusive to be a Marilyn event. Lee Strasberg gave a tribute ("Marilyn never liked goodbyes, but in the peculiar way she had of turning things around so that they faced reality—I will say au revoir"). Later DiMaggio was at some ceremony where Bobby Kennedy was shaking hands with the guests, and I was told that DiMaggio stepped out of the reception line to avoid meeting him. Bitterness ran deep now it was too late.

I know that it affected my way of seeing the Kennedys, particularly Bobby. I watched him campaigning for the Senate on the streets of New York City and within his hearing, to test him, I made a reference to Marilyn—a harmless reference, but Kennedy seemed to tense, and I heard him asking someone who I was. Friends told me that his brother's assassination had changed him and made him less tough, more thoughtful and kind. He began to quote Camus to reporters. I wasn't convinced. People in their forties don't change that easily, particularly politicians. But then he was killed. Good guys were always getting killed in the sixties, never bad guys, so Bobby must have become more good than bad. A man who worked on his presidential campaign accepted a Monroe affair as a fact, but said it had been Bobby's only one. He also said that Bobby had described her not as "a dumb broad" but as a "very remarkable girl."

I grew tired of the rumors and the speculations, my own and everybody else's. I had no wish to investigate her death. I had had some reporting experience with the Los Angeles police and they weren't the least corrupt in the world by any means. I couldn't see them pressing too hard any investigation that might involve powerful political people. While Bobby Kennedy was alive, only sly references were made in public to his involvement. He was said to have made a statement to the police, but it was kept in a secret file. Marilyn slowly slipped into the past. Her friends preferred it that way. Nothing could bring her back. Why stir up a lot of dirt? Let her memory lie undisturbed. I abandoned any idea of writing about our conversations.

But reminders kept popping up.

I met May Reis, her onetime secretary, in the Village, demonstrating against American involvement in Vietnam—that was in the very early days of the war. She showed me a small drawing Marilyn had made. Miss Reis's eyes were bright at the mention of Marilyn's name, as if she had been a beloved daughter.

A friend of Montgomery Clift's told me that *he* was very depressed. He wasn't getting many offers for movies and was haunting the New York bathhouses. It wasn't long afterward that he too was found dead in bed—not of an overdose but of a heart attack.

Lee Strasberg began sounding like Svengali. He told the *New York Times:* "I made her an actress in the way she desired to be. My wife went with her on the set and worked out her problems for her." It sounded as if Marilyn had been totally dependent on the two of them. I'm sure he didn't mean it that way, but it may have explained why she withdrew a little and turned back to Hollywood. Or had her last affair replaced the influence of the Strasbergs?

Then the lives of the Strasbergs also changed. Paula Strasberg died and Lee Strasberg remarried. The Actors Studio got backing for a Broadway season and hoped to present productions every year. If Marilyn had been alive, with her old theatrical ambitions, no doubt this would have been the time Strasberg would have tried to launch her. The studio presented a few outstanding productions, but its Broadway run was soon over and its influence consequently dimmed.

By far the most controversial theatrical event was the premiere of Arthur Miller's *After the Fall.* Elia Kazan had been put in charge of what it was hoped would become a national theater (instead, it eventually settled down to becoming a civic

218

"cultural" showpiece known as Lincoln Center—a sad story of missed opportunities that once more drove home the moral that you can't institutionalize the arts). Miller had come out of hiding and broken his silence about Marilyn. I had heard from mutual friends that he had the feeling, amounting often to tearing guilt, that the divorce had helped her toward her death and that he should have been able to do something to save her. When he had heard of her last breakdown and hospitalization and no one seemed close to her, he had been tempted to go to her rescue, but had been persuaded that he was no longer part of her life. A friend told me of his anguish and said that his new wife had persuaded him to write *After the Fall* to lay the ghost to rest and so set their own marriage free. She had my sympathy; Marilyn was a hard memory to overcome.

Miller and Kazan denied, however, that the play was about Marilyn. This was particularly hard to believe because they dressed up the actress to look as like Marilyn as possible. Miller even used the incident back in Marilyn's Hollywood career when she had had an affair with a leading Hollywood agent who was married and whose family excluded her when he died even though his last words were about her. The agent became a judge in the play and Marilyn became Maggie. "I got into the hospital before he died. But the family pushed me out and—I could hear him calling, 'Maggie . . . Maggie!' "

There are too many incidents and remarks that recall the Miller-Monroe relationship for the play not to seem a revelation of what went on behind the scenes and to be Miller's view of what went wrong.

Maggie, starting behind a switchboard, becomes not a movie star but a famous pop singer. The Miller character whom she marries (and who is the self-justifying hero of the play) is a lawyer, not a writer, and he becomes almost a father figure to her. "You're like a god!" Slowly cracks of anxiety in her begin to spoil the relationship. Maggie, who once thought she was not worthy to be his wife, either intellectually or morally ("I was with a lot of men, but I never got anything for it. It was like charity, see."), shows jealousy and also involves him in her struggle to be treated with more "respect" by her record company. When he argues with her against getting people fired, she replies: "You don't have to be ashamed of me." Call her vulgar, she tells him, since she talks like a truck driver—"Well, that's where I come from. I'm for Negroes and Puerto Ricans and truck drivers!" And he replies: "Then why do you fire people so easily?" Soon she is telling herself: "Should never have gotten married; every man I ever knew, they hate their wives." She starts to drink heavily and take pills.

When she says she intends to kill herself, he tells her: "You want to die, Maggie, and I really don't know how to prevent it." She says: "But if you loved me. . . ." and he replies: "Do you know anymore who I am? Aside from my name? I'm all the evil in the world, aren't I? All the betrayal, the broken hopes, the murderous revenge?" She wants him to take the pills from her, but he tells her: "You're trying to make me the one who does it to you. I grab them; and then we fight, and then I give them up, and you take your death from me. Something in you has been setting me up for a murder."

His feeling for her has slipped from his early admiration for her honesty ("You tell the truth, even against yourself. You're not pretending to be innocent!") to the opposite, "You eat those pills to blind yourself, but if you could only say, 'I have been cruel,' this frightening room would open. If you could say, 'I have been kicked around, but I have been just as inexcusably vicious to others, called my husband idiot in public, I have been utterly selfish despite my generosity, I have been hurt by a long line of men but I have cooperated with my persecutors—" He tells her, "no pill can make us innocent," and advises her to throw them—"death"—and all her innocence away. "See your own hatred and live!" She replies, "You tried to kill me, mister. I been killed by a lot of people, some couldn't hardly spell, but it's the same, mister." He calls an ambulance to save her from the pills. "Barbiturates kill by suffocation. And the signal is a kind of sighing—the diaphragm is paralyzed. . . ."

Miller was obviously writing out of deep personal experience and, although Maggie was only a shadow of Marilyn—the other side of Roslyn in *The Misfits*, the missing side that made her unsatisfying in the movie and hard for Monroe to make convincing—it was easy to see how Miller thought Marilyn had died, and why. But many admirers of hers were indignant at the portrait and the interpretation. James Baldwin, for example, was seen stalking up the aisle and out of the theater before the end of the play.

Even my own life had reminders of her and what we had talked about. I eventually saw Christine—whom I identified in a strange way with Marilyn, perhaps because Marilyn always asked about her and Christine admired her—when I went south to Oxford to report on James Meredith's attempt to enroll as the first black student in the University of Mississippi. Oxford was Faulkner's home town, though he had died two months before. In his last year, he had declined a dinner invitation from President Kennedy because he said it was too far to go to eat with strangers—how mad that would have made Marilyn if she'd been alive, unless by then she'd cooled on the Kennedys, too. When I reached Oxford, it was like landing in Vietnam. The U.S. Army was needed to protect Meredith. No wonder Christine was in despair. She came up to New York and talked with Malcolm X, who in those days preached regularly in Harlem at the corner of 125th Street and Seventh Avenue. Soon she didn't want to see me any more (I had one angry session with Malcolm X, at which I suppose I behaved like a "white devil"), and joined the Black Muslims. To me, the Muslims at that time seemed Christine's equivalent of Marilyn's pills. I wished then I was still seeing Marilyn for drinks because I would have liked to discuss it with her. There weren't many people I could say that about—certainly not the Maggie of Miller's play.

I also had encounters with two other people who put me in mind of Marilyn—Tennessee Williams and Marlon Brando. Williams was holed up in a hotel, not at home to anyone because he said he was going through some kind of breakdown. His recent plays had had poor reviews and short runs. I wondered what it had done to his shaky self-confidence. The only time I saw him, he seemed depressed until he became high on either liquor or pills. That was too close to Marilyn for comfort. Then I heard he'd been in a hospital and had become a Catholic and was feeling much better.

Brando was making a movie outside New York, *Reflections in a Golden Eye*, based on Carson McCullers' novel. Since it was being directed by John Huston, I went to renew acquaintances with some of the old *Misfits* people. Everybody looked a little older and nobody mentioned Marilyn. I asked the publicity man for an interview with Brando and Brando promptly took it as an opportunity for a childish temperamental outburst. Why hadn't he been told there was a reporter on the set? His rudeness was rather comic. I wondered if Marilyn had gone in for much of this kind of movie power play. Apparently she had when she felt the need to assert her star status. She had once called herself a "monster." Not long afterward,

I met Brando socially with mutual friends, and he pretended not to remember the incident. Maybe I was prejudiced, but I thought Marilyn would have been franker. Perhaps Brando had succeeded in growing a thicker skin than either Marilyn or Montgomery Clift (who was often compared with Brando) and that was why he had survived through middle age and they hadn't.

When Bobby Kennedy began his race for the presidency, I expected his enemies, many of whom were later involved in Watergate, to use the memory of Marilyn against him, but the whispers grew no louder. Perhaps after he was nominated, it would have been different—unless the Nixon strategists had already decided it might rebound against them. There were even some people who would think better of Bobby Kennedy —with his tough, ruthless image—if they knew that Marilyn Monroe had been attracted by him.

Slowly a Marilyn revival began. The magazines started using pictures of her again. Biographies came out, first referring to Kennedy anonymously as an Easterner who was a public servant and then after his death, naming him. The only point of controversy seemed to be the extent of their involvement. Opinions ranged from those of her friend, Robert Slatzer, who had no doubt that it had been "a troubled love affair that had apparently gone too far" on the basis of what Marilyn told him herself, to that of Norman Mailer, who hadn't known Marilyn but decided it must only have been a "flirtation" because Bobby Kennedy's "hard Irish nose for the real was going to keep him as celibate as the happiest priest of the county holding hands with five pretty widows." Mailer backed up his point of view by quoting Ralph Roberts, her masseur. Marilyn, Roberts recalled, had asked him, "Have you heard the rumors about Bobby and me?" and when he told her all Hollywood was talking about nothing else, she replied that it wasn't true. "I like him, but not physically." She loved his mind, she added, but did not find him as attractive as his brother. Mailer conceded that she may have been lying—I could imagine her doing it to protect Kennedy. Roberts was not an old, close friend like Slatzer, and Slatzer saw her later when she was no longer so calm. She had apparently become paranoid about the relationship, convinced that her phone was tapped, "terrified of something—or someone." Yet there were those who were convinced that the real affair had been with John Kennedy and that Bobby Kennedy had merely acted as a blind, to convince her that the affair was over and not to embarrass the President. Slatzer quotes a man (whose reliability is not established) who claimed to have seen a statement from Bobby Kennedy to the police in which Bobby Kennedy said "his brother was having wife problems because of Marilyn's calls to the White House." When Slatzer asked her if she'd ever had an affair with John Kennedy, she replied: "I'll never tell." Slatzer suggested to her that Bobby might have turned on the charm and made promises of marriage "to shake you loose." Marilyn insisted he'd meant what he said. Slatzer said he believed Kennedy had been lying. "You make me sound like a whore," Marilyn objected, and went on dreamily to ask if he could imagine her as First Lady. Slatzer gives the impression that she was in deep, and beyond a realistic assessment.

The tenth anniversary of her death was celebrated with commemorative profiles and tributes and picture spreads. I failed to see much of the woman I had come to know a little in either the pictures or the articles, which were more concerned with her image. For the first time since her death, I thought of writing about our conversations. Maybe they had some value as a glimpse of her complexity. I took my two old notebooks out of the closet and found my ancient shorthand slightly faded.

I was now inclined to take my conversations with Marilyn more seriously because of the course the public interest in her had taken. The puzzle about her death was supplanting interest in her herself and in her life. Marilyn Monroe, who in life had often been the victim of attempts to cheapen her into a dumb blonde, was now in danger of being reduced to a bit player in the continuing Kennedy saga or a murder victim in a murky Hollywood mystery. Sean O'Casey's old question—*Who killed Marilyn Monroe?*—took on a new meaning and could probably never be answered. Too many people involved were now dead or unwilling to talk. But speculation about the answer threatened to turn her complex life story into a mere whodunit.

As I had suspected at the time, the Los Angeles police investigation had not been a marvel of thoroughness. There was no coroner's inquest, even though the circumstances and contradictions in various statements seemed to call for one. It was alleged that the chief of police, William H. Parker, had been boasting that Bobby Kennedy was going to make him the next head of the FBI, and so was determined not to let the case embarrass Kennedy. Various pieces of evidence are apparently unavailable or missing—such as the alleged deposition by Kennedy and the list of Marilyn Monroe's phone calls on the day of her death. There are also disputes over the medical evidence. She died of an overdose of barbiturates, but no trace of them was found in her stomach. Was a stomach pump used to save her life by someone unknown, or was the lethal overdose injected? One doctor said that the pills could have passed into the small intestine, but this was not examined. There were other contradictions and no clear explanation. Without the clear evidence and remorseless questioning of everyone remotely concerned by a coroner's inquest, there could be no real answers, only theories. And theories abounded: she had been given a fatal injection somewhere else, to shut her embarrassing mouth for good, and then the body had been dressed up at home to look like a suicide; she had played the scene once again that Miller described in *After the Fall*—this time Bobby Kennedy was supposed to be her rescuer, only he declined to come when she called and so she died without help; Bobby Kennedy's enemies in organized crime, who are already supposed to have been tapping and bugging her house, arranged her death in such a way as to involve Kennedy, but he was too smart for them. . . .

One common theme in the theories is that Marilyn is a mere cog in some saga of the Kennedys. It was the price she paid, perhaps, for getting involved with national politicians and their world, where power is what money is to the rest of us, and individuals are no more nor less important than the power they wield. The recent CIA revelations have shown us the extent to which politics and organized crime can cross, even to using gangland killers to take care of political embarrassments. Bobby Kennedy's investigations as attorney general threatened some Mafia and union leaders, so no doubt his private life was well scrutinized. Marilyn had entered much deeper and murkier waters than she knew—at least until close to the end.

Robert Slatzer, who has shown the doggedness of an old friend in the most thorough of investigations so far, rejects the idea of suicide and seems to lean toward possible murder. He quite rightly calls for a new inquiry by the Los Angeles County authorities.

But it must be almost impossible for anyone who watched

her on *The Misfits* to accept her simply as a sordid murder victim, a pawn in someone else's power game. The way she apparently died (of an overdose at home) was a death she came close to several times. The believers in the murder theory might argue that that was the obvious way to disguise her murder, but it would be very difficult and would involve a lot of people, a lot of mouths to keep quiet. What might be called *The Misfits* theory is that all the contradictions and unanswered questions do not lead to murder. They might be answered in such a way that we see her go to the edge once too often (Marilyn as Maggie), and this time there was no Arthur Miller to pull her back. Without an inquiry to drag out the truth, we just don't know.

Richard Condon, in his novel about a presidential assassination, *Winter Kills*, dismisses murder theories about his Marilyn character (whom he depicts as involved only with the President). "Like every other suicide," writes canny ex-Hollywood press agent Condon, "she had been a suicide inside her head since she was about five years old." This is a common explanation but too pat, generally expressed by people who think suicide is wrong. People say the same about Hemingway. But Hemingway didn't commit suicide until he felt that his physical and mental deterioration had forced him to it. He had a reason, and perhaps she had. Slatzer says that when he met Marilyn close to the end, some crisis "had convulsed her very existence into a nightmare of sleeplessness and a horror that edged the borders of drug-induced delirium." Was this enough of a reason to force Marilyn Monroe to suicide, or was the crisis caused by her fear of being disposed of? Or was she playing nightmare games again, her version of Russian roulette?

The theories become like the old rumors—endless dead ends. As an old reporter, I don't like trusting other people's eyes. The reporter's ideal is the disciple, Thomas, who didn't believe in the crucifixion and resurrection until he put his hands in the wounds. Some friends like Slatzer saw, at the end, a woman under enormous stress. Other people such as her housekeeper, Eunice Murray, who apparently slept through her death, thought she was in fairly normal spirits. These conflicting versions of her state of mind would have reminded her perhaps of a quotation from Virginia Woolf—that we all may have a thousand selves. Whichever way she died, there were always murderers in her life, trying to kill off 999 of her selves and leave her as a dumb blonde. They do the same today with her memory. Of the selves I saw (at least twenty or thirty must have appeared in our conversations), the most memorable for me was the famous movie star who still had a genuine human interest in a wino in the street, concern for a sparrow among the pigeons. I have known many famous people, but none like that. Other celebrities have claimed that they were still at home in the streets, that nothing human was alien to them, but it was always only an act; they behaved with condescension. With that self of hers, it was genuine, perhaps the positive side of that damned inferiority complex that had so many negative effects on her life. Perhaps she sensed that she was still safer with those kinds of people than with most of those she mixed with after she became famous.

I recently went back to that bar on Eighth Avenue—I had avoided that part of the city for many years—and everything looked different, much greyer and rundown, closed or renovated. The bar had been between 43rd and 44th or 44th and 45th Streets—I could no longer remember which—and I wasn't sure I could recognize it now. It made me realize how long ago it was—nearly a decade and a half. I walked by the Actors Studio, and that seemed much dimmer and more depressing than I remembered. The trouble was, you didn't really know if the places had changed all that much or whether it was only you. But at least one person would never change now, would never grow old. What was it she had told me in the bar so long ago? "Sometimes I think it would be easier to avoid old age, to die young, but then you'd never complete your life, would you? You'd never wholly know yourself. . . ."